NUTCASES

HUMAN RIGHTS

Other Titles in the Series

Constitutional and
Administrative Law
Contract Law
Criminal Law
Employment Law
European Union Law
Equity & Trusts
Land Law
Tort

Titles in the Nutshell Series

A Level Law
Administrative Law
Company Law
Consumer Law
Contract Law
Constitutional Law
Criminal Law
Employment Law
English Legal System
European Union Law
Equity and Trusts
Evidence
Family Law
Human Rights
Land Law
Tort
Trusts

AUSTRALIA
Law Book Co.
Sydney

CANADA and USA
Carswell
Toronto

HONG KONG
Sweet & Maxwell Asia

NEW ZEALAND
Brookers
Wellington

SINGAPORE and MALAYSIA
Sweet & Maxwell Asia
Singapore and Kuala Lumpur

NUTCASES

HUMAN RIGHTS

FIRST EDITION

by

MAUREEN SPENCER
Principal Lecturer in Law, Middlesex University

and

JOHN SPENCER
Barrister

London ● Sweet & Maxwell ● 2002

Published in 2002 by
Sweet & Maxwell Limited of
100 Avenue Road, London, NW3 3PF
(http://www.sweetandmaxwell.co.uk)
Typeset by LBJ Typesetting Ltd of Kingsclere
Printed in Great Britain by Creative Print and Design
(Wales) Ebbw Vale

No natural forests were destroyed to make
this product; only farmed timber
was used and replanted

A CIP Catalogue record for this book
is available from the British Library

ISBN 0–421–767308

©
Sweet & Maxwell
2002

CONTENTS

CONTENTS

TABLE OF CASES

1. SOURCES OF HUMAN RIGHTS LAW

ECHR and Responsibility of the State

Key Principle: Article 1 of the European Convention on Human Rights: "The High Contracting Parties shall secure to everyone within their jurisdiction the rights and freedoms defined in Section 1 of this Convention"

Key Principle: A state must provide a legal framework to protect Convention rights effectively.

Young, James and Webster v. U.K.

British Rail and three trade unions had agreed a "closed shop" condition whereby membership of one of the unions became a condition of employment with British Rail. The three applicants had been working for British Rail before the date of the agreement. They refused to join one of the unions on political and conscientious grounds. They could not claim protection on the sole ground of exemption from union membership, namely religious belief. They alleged breaches of Articles 9,10,11 and 13.

Held: (ECtHR) The State was responsible for allowing the violations since Article 1 requires each Contracting State to secure Convention rights for those within its jurisdiction. (1981) 4 E.H.R.R. 38

Commentary

The court considered that it was not material to the case that British Rail was a public body. The obligation would have applied if a private body had been the employer, since "it was the domestic law in force at the relevant time that made lawful the treatment of which the applicants complained. The responsibility of the Respondent State for any resultant breach of the Convention is thus engaged". Article 1 has not been incorporated under

the Human Rights Act 1998 (HRA). This is arguably understand-
able since the Government has assumed the responsibility referred
to in the Article by passing the Act. On the other hand the
omission has implications for the obligation to uphold Convention
rights in the private law sphere. The European Court of Human
Rights, as this case indicates, imposed a responsibility on states for
violations by private bodies by citing Article 1. (See pp. 30–32 for
more recent cases on the obligations of private bodies).

Judicial Reasoning

Key Principle: **Articles 8, 9, 10 and 11 of the European
Convention on Human Rights allow limitations that are, *inter
alia*, prescribed by law.**

Hashman and Harrup v. U.K.
The applicants, hunt saboteurs, had blown a horn with the
intention of disrupting a hunt. This was not an unlawful act,
there was no threat of violence and no breach of the peace. It
was likely that behaviour would have been reported. They were
bound over to be of good behaviour under the Justices of the
Peace Act 1361. They claimed breaches of Articles 10,11 and 5.
The Commission declared admissibility under Articles 10 and
11.

Held: (ECtHR) The applicants' behaviour was an expression of
opinion within the meaning of Article 10. The measures taken
interfered with their right to freedom of expression and the
interference was not "prescribed by law" within the meaning of
Article 10(2). Conduct *contra bonos mores* was defined in English
law as behaviour which was "wrong rather than right in the
judgement of the majority of contemporary fellow citizens".
This definition did not give sufficiently clear guidance, and was
too imprecise and unpredictable in its operation to satisfy
Article 10(2). (2000) 30 E.H.R.R. 241

Steel and Others v. U.K.
The applicants were arrested and detained as a consequence of
being engaged in various forms of public protest. They were
charged with conduct likely to cause a breach of the peace. The
first applicant walked in front of a member of a grouse shoot as
he lifted his shotgun and was committed to prison for 28 days

when she refused to be bound over to keep the peace following a finding that the case against her was proved. She was convicted of breach of the peace and an offence contrary to section 5 of the Public Order Act 1994. In respect of the former offence the magistrates did not specify what behaviour justified the conclusion. The second applicant was arrested after protesting against the extension of a motorway. She stood under a digger, was arrested for conduct likely to cause a breach of the peace and was committed to prison for seven days after refusing to be bound over. The other three applicants were detained by police for seven hours after attending a "Fighter Helicopter 11" conference to protest against the sale of fighter helicopters. They had held up banners saying "Work for Peace not War". They were taken into custody where the custody record stated the "circumstances" as being that they were acting in breach of the peace. They were detained for seven hours. The proceedings against them were dropped when the prosecution decided not to call any evidence. They all complained that their arrest and detention had not been "prescribed by law" as set out in Article 5(1) since the concept of breach of the peace and the power to bind over were not sufficiently clearly defined. There were breaches, they alleged, of Article 5(5) because of the magistrates' immunity from civil proceedings. They stated that because of the uncertainty inherent in the concept of breach of the peace and the power to bind over and the fact that their detention was a disproportionate response that their rights under Articles 10 and 11 were infringed.

Held: (ECtHR) The concept of breach of the peace was sufficiently clarified by the English courts to satisfy the requirement of "prescribed by law" under Article 10(2) and was formulated with sufficient precision to satisfy Article 5(1)(a). There was no breach of Articles 5(1) or 10 in respect of the first two applicants. There had been violations of Article 10 in respect of the third, fourth and fifth applicants since the arrests and detention were not "prescribed by law" in that they were disproportionate to the aim of preventing disorder or protecting the rights of others. There were no breaches of Article 5(5). (1998) 28 E.H.R.R. 603

Commentary

In *Steel* the court considered that the law in relation to breach of the peace was sufficiently precise and with foreseeable legal consequences to satisfy Article 5(1) and thus appeared to give the member state some scope for interpretation although the judgment itself does not refer to margin of appreciation. However the term *contra bonos mores*, meaning contrary to a good way of life, set out in the Justices of the Peace Act 1361, was too imprecise as the *Harrup* decision stated. In *McLeod v. U.K.* (1999) 27 E.H.R.R. 493 the European Court of Human Rights also found that the breach of the peace doctrine was in accordance with the law under Article 8 although the police response was disproportionate. The key factors in defining legal basis are certainty and accessibility. The principle of legality is upheld also in the alternative phrasing "in accordance with law". In *Silver v. U.K.* (1983) 5 E.H.R.R. 347 the court accepted that lawfulness may be based on the exercise of judicial discretion but there must be sufficient indication of the circumstances in which the discretion will be exercised. In *Malone v. U.K.* (1985) 7 E.H.R.R. 14 the court held that any restriction must be certain and reasonably foreseeable, but also commented that "the requirements of foreseeability cannot mean that an individual should be enabled to foresee when the authorities are likely to intercept his communications so that he can adapt his conduct accordingly".

Key Principle: **Permissible restrictions of Convention rights must be proportionate.**

R. v. Lambert

The appellant was convicted of the offence of possessing a controlled drug of class A with intent to supply, contrary to section 5(3) of the Misuse of Drugs Act 1971. His trial had taken place before the HRA came into force. In his defence he had relied on section 28(3)(b)(1) of that Act asserting that he did not believe or have reason to suspect that the bag which he carried contained a controlled drug. The judge had directed the jury to the effect that the prosecutors had to prove (1) that he had the bag in his possession; (2) that he knew that he had the bag in his possession and (3) that the bag contained a controlled drug. To establish a defence under the section the defendant had to prove on the balance of probabilities that he did not know the bag contained a controlled drug. Such was the accepted law at the time. The appeal was on the grounds that the requirement to prove the defence on the balance of probabilities was contrary to the presumption of innocence guaranteed under Article 6 of the European Convention on Human Rights. The Court of Appeal dismissed the appeal. There was an appeal to the House of Lords. The court also certified as a point of law whether a defendant whose trial took place before sections 6 and 7(1)(b) of the HRA were in force was entitled once they were in force to rely on an alleged breach of his Convention rights by the trial court or prosecuting authority. The appellant contended that he was so entitled and also that section 6 of the HRA meant that the House of Lords as a public authority sitting in judgment once the Act was in force could not affirm convictions obtained in breach of such rights before October 2, 2000.

Held: (HL) It was not justifiable or a proportionate response to the problem of illegal drugs to transfer the legal burden on the accused and require him to prove on the balance of probabilities that he did not know the bag contained a controlled drug. It was however possible using section 3 of the HRA to interpret section 28 as imposing an evidential burden only. Such a requirement was not a violation of the Convention. If the trial judge had given the direction to the jury that the accused had only the evidential burden the jury would have reached the same conclusion. The conviction should therefore stand. Furthermore the HRA was not available to the applicant since his conviction predated its coming into force. [2001] 3 W.L.R. 206

Commentary
The word proportionate does not appear in the text of the Convention. It relates to the application of the requirements for restrictions in rights to be "necessary in a democratic society", implying the existence of a "pressing social need" (see *Handyside v. U.K.* (1976) 1 E.H.R.R. 737). The concept is most often applied in considering the restrictions of rights under Articles 8–11 but also applies to Article 6, as here, Articles 5 and 12, and Article 1 of the First Protocol. Roderick Munday has commented that "*Lambert* neatly illustrates the unpredictability of the human rights notion of proportionality" (*Evidence*, Butterworth's Core Text Series, 2001, p. 65). He points out that in such cases "European human rights law becomes an instrument enabling the courts to appraise and even override what have traditionally been considered essentially political decisions". The differing decisions of the Court of Appeal and the House of Lords illustrate contradictory views on the extent to which the State should be allowed to undermine the rights of defendants in the interests of protecting society against the dangers of drug dealing.

Key Principle: **States should be allowed some measure of freedom, or a margin of appreciation in applying the Convention.**

Handyside v. U.K.
The applicant was convicted under the Obscene Publications Acts 1959 and 1964. He was the owner of a publishers which published a book, *The Little Red Schoolbook*, which included a section on sex, covering topics such as masturbation, menstruation and pornography. He claimed a violation of Article 10.

Held: (ECtHR) There was no uniform European concept of morals and state authorities were in a better position to assess the situation than international judges. There was no violation of Article 10 since the interference with the applicant's freedom of expression was necessary in a democratic society, "for the protection of morals". The United Kingdom had acted in good faith within the limits of the margin of appreciation allowed. [1976] 1 E.H.R.R. 737

Commentary
The book had been published in Denmark in 1969 and then in a number of other countries including Belgium, France, Greece, Iceland, Italy, Norway and Sweden. There had been no criminal proceedings anywhere else. The close connection between the concepts of proportionality and margin of appreciation is illustrated also in *Gay News and Lemon v. U.K.* (1983) 5 E.H.R.R. 123 where the Commission considered the application of the law of blasphemous libel. In finding that there was no violation of Article 10 in a private prosecution against a publisher and editor for vilifying Christ, the Commission stated "it is in principle left to the legislature of the State concerned how it wishes to define the offence, provided that the principle of proportionality which is inherent in the exception clause of Article 10(2) is being respected". In *R. v. DPP, ex parte Kebilene* (see also pp. 26, 80) Lord Hope stated that "by conceding a margin of appreciation to each national system the court has recognised that the Convention, as a living system, doesn't need to be applied uniformly by all states but may vary in its application according to local needs and conditions. This technique is not available to the national courts when they are considering Convention issues arising within their own countries". As Lord Hope's statement indicates, national

courts are not required to consider the doctrine of margin of appreciation in applying the Convention. In domestic law the doctrine of proportionality is sufficient to allow an assessment of the appropriateness of a policy decision by the executive. However, when they take into account the Strasbourg cases involving other member states the English courts will doubtless apply the cases with an awareness that other countries may operate in a different cultural and ethical context. If however there is a resort to a particular legal approach in a large number of other countries this gives an indication that it is one of more universal validity and "necessary in a democratic society".

Smith and Grady v. U.K.

United Kingdom government policy was that homosexuality was incompatible with service in the armed forces and that personnel known to be homosexual or engaging in homosexual activity would be administratively discharged. The applicants were serving members of the armed forces who had been administratively discharged because of their homosexuality. The Court of Appeal had dismissed their applications for judicial review of the decision to discharge. They claimed violations of Articles 8 and 3.

Held: (ECtHR) The discharges were in violation of Articles 8 and 13. The Court of Appeal's application of the test of irrationality placed the threshold so high as to preclude consideration of proportionality and whether pressing social need existed for the ban on homosexuals. [2000] 29 E.H.R.R. 493

Commentary

The Court of Appeal had been ready to apply a lower threshold of unreasonableness in a case such as this involving human rights but on the facts had found against the applicants. By contrast the European Court of Human Rights although recognising that in pursuing the aim of national security the state was entitled to a broader margin of appreciation, emphasised that when a state infringes "a most intimate aspect of an individual's private life particularly serious reasons by way of justification [are] required".

Key Principle: **The Convention is a living instrument and must be interpreted in the light of present day conditions.**

Tyrer v. U.K.
The 15-year-old applicant had been sentenced to three strokes of
the birch in the Isle of Man for unlawful assault. This was
administered in a police station. He was held down by two
policemen while a third birched him. He claimed a violation of
Article 3 of European Convention on Human Rights. The
Government relied on Article 63(3) of the Convention and
argued that since public opinion in the Isle of Man supported
birching it was a "local requirement".

Held: (ECtHR) Judicial corporal punishment was degrading
within the meaning of Article 3. The task of the European Court
of Human Rights was to develop the rules instituted by the
Convention which must be regarded as a living instrument. The
Convention should not be interpreted as it would have been by
those who drafted it but "must be interpreted in the light of
present day conditions". (1978) 2 E.H.R.R. 1

Commentary
This principle allows the meaning attached to articles to change
over time but old cases do not have to be specifically overruled.
There is no doctrine of precedent under the Convention although
the court will usually follow its previous decisions. However, older
decisions may be disregarded in the light of new conditions. For
example, in a case involving the rights of transsexuals (*Sheffield
and Horsham v. U.K.* (1999) 5 B.H.R.C. 83) the European
Convention on Human Rights noted the changing attitudes in this
area compared to a situation involving a previous case (*Cossey v.
U.K.* (1990) 13 E.H.R.R. 622). There was now "an increased
social acceptance of transsexuals" and "the Court reiterated that
this area needs to be kept under review by the contracting state".
See also pp. 126–130, 141–143.

Derogations

Key Principle: **Article 15(1) of the European Convention on
Human Rights: "In time of war or other public emergency
threatening the life of the nation any High Contracting Party
may take measures derogating from its obligations under this**

Convention to the extent strictly required by the exigencies of the situation, provided that such measures are not inconsistent with its other obligations under international law."

Brannigan and McBride v. U.K.

The applicants had been arrested and detained in Northern Ireland under the provisions of the Prevention of Terrorism (Temporary Provisions) Act 1984 (PTA). Brannigan was detained for six days, 14 hours and 30 minutes and McBride for four days, six hours and 25 minutes. Both were interrogated, denied access to reading and writing materials and access to a solicitor was delayed for 48 hours. The applicants relied on the *Brogan* case (see p. 59), the Government relied on its derogation under Article 15 which purported to authorise further detention of suspected terrorists for questioning without charge.

Held: (ECtHR) There was a breach of Article 5, paragraph 3, but the derogation lodged by the United Kingdom satisfied the requirements of Article 15. [1994] 17 E.H.R.R. 539

Commentary

The European Court of Human Rights noted that the remedy of habeas corpus was available to test the lawfulness of the original arrest and detention and that the detainees had an absolute and legally enforceable right to consult a solicitor after 48 hours from the time of arrest. It considered that the Government had not exceeded its margin of appreciation in deciding for executive rather than judicial control of the extension of the period of detention. The HRA, Sched. 3, sets out the text of this derogation. The United Kingdom entered the derogation after the case of *Brogan v. U.K.* (1988) 11 E.H.R.R. 117 in which the court held that the detention of the applicants under the PTA for more than four days without charge was a breach of Article 5(3). The Government wished to preserve the Secretary of State's power under the PTA to extend the period of detention of persons suspected of terrorism in connection with Northern Ireland for a total of up to seven days. Section 14 of the HRA lists "designated derogations" which can be continued for up to five years. No derogations may be made for Article 2, except in respect of deaths resulting from lawful acts of war, or for Articles 3 or 4. The United Kingdom has entered further derogation for Article 5 in relation to the provisions of the Anti-Terrorism, Crime and Security Bill 2001.

Other International Obligations

Key Principle: **The United Kingdom has treaty obligations to change the law so as to comply with human rights key obligations under the European Convention on Human Rights.**

The Sunday Times v. United Kingdom

The Sunday Times brought an action before the European Commission on Human Rights claiming that the injunction upheld by the House of Lords [1974] A.C. 273 infringed their right to freedom of expression guaranteed by Article 10 of the European Convention on Human Rights. The Commission referred the case to the Court of Human Rights.

Held: (ECtHR) The interference with the applicant's freedom of expression was not justified under Article 10(2) which permitted such restrictions "as are prescribed by law and are necessary in a democratic society. . .for maintaining the authority and impartiality of the judiciary". There was no "pressing social need" for the injunction. [1979] 2 E.H.R.R. 245

Commentary

This is one example where the United Kingdom has introduced legislation to implement the court's decisions. The judgment led to the Contempt of Court Act 1981.

Key Principle: **International treaty obligations may provide guidance when a court is called upon to interpret an ambiguous statute.**

R. v. Secretary of State for Home Department, ex parte Brind

The Secretary of State made orders under the Broadcasting Act 1981 banning television and radio stations from broadcasting the words spoken by spokesmen of organisations proscribed under anti-terrorism legislation. Broadcasters sought judicial review of the orders as being outside the Secretary of State's powers because the ban was disproportionate to its ostensible object of preventing intimidation by the organisations concerned and also because he should have regard to the European Convention on Human Rights. The application was dismissed by the Divisional Court and by the Court of Appeal. The broadcasters appealed.

Held: (HL) The presumption that Parliament had intended to legislate in conformity with the European Convention might be resorted to in order to resolve ambiguities in a statute, but in the present case there was no ambiguity and no presumption that the Secretary of State had to exercise his discretion under the Act in accordance with the Convention. [1991] 1 A.C. 696

Commentary
Lord Ackner said that since there was no ambiguity in the relevant section of the statute there was no need here to have recourse to the Convention. He said that the limits placed upon discretion were that the power should be used for the purpose for which it was granted and that it must be exercised reasonably in the *Wednesbury* sense (*Associated Provincial Picture Houses Ltd v. Wednesbury Corporation* [1948] 1 K.B. 223). He also referred to Lord Denning's judgment in *R. v. Chief Immigration Officer, ex parte Salamat Bibi* [1976] 1 W.L.R. 979 where he said: "the position as I understand it is that if there is any ambiguity in our statutes, or uncertainty in our law, then this Court can look to the Convention as an aid to clear up the ambiguity and uncertainty." The status of the European Convention in United Kingdom law has been changed as a result of the HRA. From October 2000 the courts must "take into account" the judgments of the Court of Human Rights and the opinions of the former European Commission on Human Rights. This on its wording has a stronger meaning than calling on the Convention as an aid to interpretation in cases of ambiguity. The status of the other treaty obligations is unchanged by the HRA but in practice they are far less often at issue. In *Brind v. United Kingdom* (1994) 77–A D.R. 42 the Commission rejected the journalists' contention that there was a violation of Article 10. The ban was proportionate in view of the need to combat terrorism. This decision illustrates that in some instances the incorporation of the Convention may be unlikely to have any effect on existing English law. A number of commentators are critical of the position that international treaties can only be relied on as sources of law where legislation is ambiguous. For example Murray Hunt has argued:

> "in short, English courts have been asking the wrong question. Instead of asking, 'Is the domestic law ambiguous?' they should have

been asking 'Can the domestic law be read in a way which avoids a conflict with international law?' To answer that question properly, it will always be necessary for the domestic court to have regard to the terms of those obligations, without first having to undertake the wholly artificial exercise of construing domestic law in isolation to determine whether it is 'ambiguous'."

(Murray Hunt, *Using Human Rights Law in English Courts*, Hart Publishing 1998, p. 39). The United Kingdom is signatory to a number of international human rights treaties apart from the European Convention on Human Rights. These include the Universal Declaration of Human Rights, the International Covenant on Civil and Political Rights and the International Covenant on Economic Social and Cultural Rights. In *R. v. Secretary of State for the Environment, ex parte NALGO* (1992) 5 Admin. L.R. 785 the court stated that human rights treaties may be used where the relevant rules of common law or equity are uncertain. Along with *Brind* this is a controversial principle since it appears to state that administrative decision makers are only obliged to take account of international human rights treaties if the common law or statute is unclear. However on a more positive note Neill L.J. stated that human rights treaties "may be used when the court is considering how a discretion is to be exercised", for example in deciding whether to grant an interlocutory injunction.

Key Principle: **There is a body of customary international law which is part of the common law.**

R. v. Bow Street Metropolitan Stipendiary Magistrate, ex parte Pinochet Ugarte (No. 3)
For facts see p. 47.

Held: (HL) Though a former head of state had immunity from the criminal jurisdiction of the United Kingdom for acts done in his official capacity as head of state, torture was an international crime against humanity and there was a universal jurisdiction to extradite or punish a public official for torture. That principle extended to heads of state because the state parties who had created the international jurisdiction by the International Convention against Torture, Inhuman or Degrading Treatment could not have intended to create an immunity for a head of state who was a torturer. *Per* Lords Millett and Phillips the systematic use of torture was an international crime against humanity for which there could be no immunity even before the International Convention came into effect, consequently there was no immunity under customary international law for the offences relating to torture alleged against the applicant. [1999] 2 W.L.R. 827

Commentary
This case demonstrates how increasingly English judges are drawing on human rights cases from other jurisdictions in their judgments. Similarly in *R. v. Lambert* Lord Steyn cited Canadian and South African human rights cases; see p. 4.

2. HUMAN RIGHTS ACT 1998

Interpretation

Key Principle: **Section 3 of the HRA—Interpretation of legislation:**

"(1) So far as it is possible to do so, primary legislation and subordinate legislation must be read and given effect in a way which is compatible with the Convention rights.

(2) This section—

    (a) applies to primary legislation and subordinate legislation whenever enacted;

    (b) does not affect the validity, continuing operation or enforcement of any incompatible subordinate legislation if (disregarding any possibility of revocation) primary legislation prevents removal of the incompatibility."

Key Principle: **Courts must adopt a purposive approach to interpretation of legislation to ensure compliance with the ECHR.**

R. v. Offen

The appellant had been given an automatic life sentence under section 2 of the Crime (Sentences) Act 1997 following conviction for robbery. Under this section automatic life sentences should be imposed in such cases of repeat offenders unless there were "exceptional circumstances". It was argued that this section should be construed in the light of the interpretive provisions of section 3 of the HRA or a declaration of incompatibility should be made.

Held: (CA) The purpose behind the section was protection of the public and the fact that an offender did not pose a considerable threat to the public amounted to an "exceptional circumstance" under section 2. The court did not have to impose a life sentence. If a life sentence had been necessary this would not contravene the ECHR provided section 2 was interpreted in a way which safeguarded the public. [2001] 1 W.L.R. 253

Commentary

This was an early example of how the courts have adopted a creative approach to interpretation of legislation to avoid declarations of incompatibility. See Chapter 4 for other cases dealing with the problem of the role of the courts in sentencing.

Key Principle: **In applying a statutory provision in the light of the ECHR it may sometimes be necessary to adopt an interpretation which may appear to be linguistically strained.**

R. v. A. (No. 2)

The defendant had been charged with rape. He had claimed that sexual intercourse with the complainant had been by consent and that they had had a prior sexual relationship for about three weeks. At a pre-trial hearing the judge, relying on section 41 of the Youth Justice and Criminal Evidence Act 1999, had ruled that the complainant could not be cross-examined and that evidence could not be led about her alleged sexual relationship with the defendant. The defendant appealed against the decision. The Court of Appeal allowed the appeal and conveyed the following question to the House of Lords: "May a sexual relationship between a defendant and complainant be relevant to the issue of consent so as to render its exclusion under section

41 Youth Justice and Criminal Evidence Act 1999 a contravention of the defendant's right to a fair trial?"

Held: (HL) Section 41 of the 1999 Act should be read in accordance with section 3 of the HRA 1998 and given effect in a way that was compatible with the fair trial guaranteed under Article 6 ECHR. [2001] 2 W.L.R. 1546

Commentary
This case illustrates the new interpretative technique introduced by the HRA. The House of Lords considered that the defendant's prior relations with the complainant, although they may be relevant, could not be admitted under normal canons of statutory interpretation under section 41 of the Youth Justice and Criminal Evidence Act. The House avoided making a declaration of incompatibility by interpreting the section in a manner compatible with the demands of Article 6 of the Convention. Lord Steyn (at para. 44) made it clear that the courts should not imply the word "reasonable" into section 3. In other words they should find a possible not necessarily a reasonable interpretation according to the wording. It is arguable however that the kind of creative juridical reasoning adopted here flouts the will of Parliament. The courts are in these cases developing an approach to demarcate between section 3 interpretive technique and incompatibility under section 4. In *Donoghue v. Poplar Housing and Regeneration Association* [2001] 3 W.L.R. 183 Lord Woolf stated that "Section 3 does not enable the courts to legislate; its task is still one of interpretation but interpretation in conjunction with the direction contained in Section 3". In *R. v. A.* Lord Steyn's liberal interpretation of section 3(1) of the HRA was in part based on the desirability of avoiding making a declaration of incompatibility. He said that such a declaration would only occur if "a clear limitation on Convention rights is stated in terms. . ." The position Lord Steyn is putting forward suggests that he would only make a declaration of incompatibility if the statute stated expressly that it was limiting Convention rights. Such an occurrence would be very rare.

Key Principle: **Section 2 of the HRA—Interpretation of Convention rights:**

"(1) A court or tribunal determining a question which has arisen in connection with a Convention right must take into account any—

(a) judgment, decision, declaration or advisory opinion
of the European Court of Human Rights;
(b) opinion of the Commission given in a report adopted
under Article 31 of the Convention;
(c) decision of the Commission in connection with Article 26 or 27(2) of the Convention; or
(d) decision of the Committee of Ministers taken under
Article 46 of the Convention,

whenever made or given, so far as, in the opinion of the
court or tribunal, it is relevant to the proceedings in which
that question has arisen.

(2) Evidence of any judgment, decision, declaration or opinion of which account may have to be taken under this
section is to be given in proceedings before any court or
tribunal in such a manner as may be provided by the
rules.

(3) In this section 'rules' means rules of court or, in the case
of proceedings before a tribunal, rules made for the
purposes of this section—

(a) by the Lord Chancellor or the Secretary of State, in
relation to any proceedings outside Scotland;
(b) by the Secretary of State, in relation to proceedings in
Scotland; or
(c) by a Northern Ireland department, in relation to
proceedings before a tribunal in Northern Ireland—

(i) which deals with transferred matters; and
(ii) for which no rules made under paragraph (a) are
in force."

Key Principle: **When scrutinising executive decisions that
interfere with human rights the courts must take into account
the European jurisprudence in accordance with section 2 of
the 1998 Act.**

R. (Mahmood) v. Secretary of State for the Home Department
The applicant was an illegal immigrant married to a British
citizen who had had his asylum claim refused. He applied for
leave to remain on the basis of his marriage. This was refused.
The applicant applied for judicial review of the Secretary of
State's decisions.

Held: (CA) Appeal dismissed. The case should be approached as if the Act had been in force when the Secretary of State reached his decision since it involved fundamental rights including the right to family life under Article 8. In considering the test of necessity in this context the court must take into account the European jurisprudence. There were reasonable grounds for concluding that the applicant's deportation was necessary in the interests of an orderly and fair control of immigration and that his right to family life was not violated. [2001] 1 W.L.R. 840

Commentary

Under section 21 of the HRA Strasbourg jurisprudence is persuasive but not legally binding. In *R. (Alconbury Developments Ltd) v. The Secretary of State for the Environment, Transport and the Regions* (see p. 104) Lord Hoffman stated: "The House is not bound by the decisions of the European Court and, if I thought that the Divisional Court was right (it was not) to hold that they compelled a conclusion fundamentally at odds with the distribution of powers under the British constitution I would have considerable doubt as to whether they should be followed." British judges in particular have been critical of the Strasbourg judgment in *Osman v. U.K.* (1999) 29 E.H.R.R. 245, (see p. 35). In practice the United Kingdom courts have followed the interpretation of the ECHR. at Strasbourg. Of course the Strasbourg decisions can be interpreted differently or there may be no Strasbourg decision on the case in point (see *R. (DPP) v. Havering Magistrates* [2001] 1 W.L.R. 805, pp. 61–62). One issue in that case was whether the provisions of Article 5 include a requirement that underlying facts relevant to detention are to be proved to the criminal standard of proof. Latham L.J. stated:

> "It is true that the European Court of Human Rights on occasion refers to the need for evidence; but that is used in contradistinction to a mere assertion. It does not seem to me that any of the authorities to which we have been referred assist in determining the nature of that 'evidence'. Bearing in mind the differences in the rules for admissibility of evidence in their different jurisdictions of the Member States, it is perhaps not surprising that the court appears to have left resolution of that question to domestic law".

He drew on authorities from English law in this case.

Declarations of Incompatibility

Key Principle: **Section 4 of the HRA—Declaration of incompatibility:**

"(1) Subsection (2) applies in any proceedings in which a court determines whether a provision of primary legislation is compatible with a Convention right.

(2) If the court is satisfied that the provision is incompatible with a Convention right, it may make a declaration of that incompatibility.

(3) Subsection (4) applies in any proceedings in which a court determines whether a provision of subordinate legislation, made in the exercise of a power conferred by primary legislation, is compatible with a Convention right.

(4) If the court is satisfied—

(a) that the provision is incompatible with a Convention right, and

(b) that (disregarding any possibility of revocation) the primary legislation concerned prevents removal of the incompatibility,

it may make a declaration of that incompatibility.

(5) In this section 'court' means—

(a) the House of Lords;

(b) the Judicial Committee of the Privy Council;

(c) the Courts-Martial Appeal Court;

(d) in Scotland, the High Court of Justiciary sitting otherwise than as a trial court or the Court of Session;

(e) in England and Wales or Northern Ireland, the High Court or the Court of Appeal.

(6) A declaration under this section ('a declaration of incompatibility')—

(a) does not affect the validity, continuing operation or enforcement of the provision in respect of which it is given; and

(b) is not binding on the parties to the proceedings in which it is made."

Key Principle: **If the words used in the structure are so clear that interpretative techniques of section 3 of the HRA cannot provide a method of finding compatibility a declaration of incompatibility will be made, but as a last resort.**

Wilson v. First County Trust Fund

The claimant and a firm of pawnbrokers had made a credit agreement for a loan. A BMW car was proffered as security. There was a technical fault in the agreement and as a result it was unenforceable by virtue of section 127 of the Consumer Credit Act 1974. The issue was whether the section was incompatible with the right to property in Protocol 1, Article 1. The Secretary of State intervened arguing that the act complained of occurred before the HRA came into force and so the court should not consider the issue.

Held: (CA) A declaration of incompatibility should be made. The court had to act in a way which was compatible with the Convention and so the fact that the agreement pre-dated the operation of the HRA was irrelevant. There was a violation of Article 6 which guarantees a fair hearing for the determination of civil rights and obligations since although the creditor had rights they were unenforceable. The creditor also suffered a disproportionate violation of his property rights. It was not possible to "read down" the Consumer Credit Act in terms of the HRA. [2001] 3 All E.R. 229

R. (H) v. Mental Health Tribunal North and East London Region 2001

Section 73 of the Mental Health Act 1983 states that a restricted patient should be discharged if the tribunal is satisfied that certain conditions apply and it is not appropriate to continue with treatment. The conditions include that he is not suffering from mental illness and it is not necessary for him to receive treatment either for his benefit or for the safety of others. The question was on whom was the burden of proof that the conditions were satisfied. If the patient was not to be discharged unless the tribunal was satisfied as to the conditions this arguably would reverse the burden of proof and be a breach of Article 5 whereby a person could only be detained in accordance with the law.

Held: (CA) Section 73 of the 1983 Act was incompatible with the HRA. The Convention required that the discharge should be

ordered unless the criteria were made out. Section 73 did not
provide this. [2001] 3 W.L.R. 42

Commentary
The House of Lords granted leave to appeal in *Wilson*. It is
arguable that the courts will in future take a different approach to
declarations of incompatibility in the light of the House of Lords
decision of *R. v. A.* (see p. 14). The Divisional Court in *R.
(Alconbury Developments Ltd) v. Secretary of State for the Environment, Transport and the Regions* declared a declaration of incompatibility. The ruling was made in respect of four planning cases
but the declaration was reversed by the House of Lords on the
grounds that a close reading of the Convention case-law revealed
that no incompatibility arose. (See p. 104).

Key Principle: **Section 5 of the HRA—Right of Crown to
intervene:**

"(1) Where a court is considering whether to make a declaration of incompatibility, the Crown is entitled to notice in
accordance with rules of court.

(2) In any case to which subsection (1) applies—

(a) a Minister of the Crown (or a person nominated by
him),
(b) a member of the Scottish Executive,
(c) a Northern Ireland Minister,
(d) a Northern Ireland department,
is entitled, on giving notice in accordance with rules
of court, to be joined as a party to the proceedings.

(3) Notice under subsection (2) may be given at any time
during the proceedings.

(4) A person who has been made a party to criminal proceedings (other than in Scotland) as the result of a notice
under subsection (2) may, with leave, appeal to the House
of Lords against any declaration of incompatibility made
in the proceedings.

(5) In subsection (4)—

'criminal proceedings' includes all proceedings
before the Courts-Martial Appeal Court; and

'leave' means leave granted by the Court making the declaration of incompatibility or by the House of Lords.''

Key Principle: **The purpose of section 5 in conferring on a minister the right to be heard was to ensure that the relevant minister had the opportunity to participate in the hearing.**

R. v. A. (No. 1)
For background facts see p. 14.

There was no proposal by the parties that during the course of the appeal the House should be asked to consider making a declaration of incompatibility. Accordingly the circumstances had not arisen for applying the proceedings prescribed by Directions 30.2 and 30.4 of the House of Lords Practice Directions and standing orders applicable to Criminal Appeals on the hearing of such an issue. The Home Secretary nevertheless petitioned for leave to intervene.

Held: (HL) Although as a general rule the effect on the fairness of a trial of the admission or exclusion of evidence was to be judged after its completion in the context of the proceedings as a whole, it was undesirable that the vulnerable witness, the complainant, should be exposed to the risk of having to give evidence again if the trial was found to be unfair. The issue of incompatibility was one of general public importance and it was in the best interests of all the parties that the issue should be determined in advance of the trial and without delay. The Secretary of State who had borne responsibility for the promotion of the Youth Justice and Criminal Evidence Act 1999 should be joined as a party to the proceedings. [2001] 1 W.L.R. 789

Commentary
The House considered that although the Crown was an appellant and represented by the Director his role as prosecutor was different from that of a minister with executive responsibilities.

Key Principle: **Section 19 of the HRA—Statements of compatibility:**

"(1) A Minister of the Crown in charge of a Bill in either House of Parliament must, before a Second Reading of the Bill—

    (a) make a statement to the effect that in his view the provisions of the Bill are compatible with the Convention rights ('a statement of compatibility'); or

    (b) make a statement to the effect that although he is unable to make a statement of compatibility the government nevertheless wishes the House to proceed with the Bill.

(2) The statement must be in writing and be published in such manner as the Minister making it considers appropriate."

Key Principle: **Statements of compatibility are not binding on the courts.**

R. v. A.
For facts and holding see p. 14.

Commentary
Statements of compatibility are, according to Lord Hope, no more than expressions of opinion by the minister. Counsel for the Secretary of State did not rely on the statement in the course of argument.

Retrospectivity

Key Principle: **(1) Section 7 of the HRA—Proceedings:**

"(1) A person who claims that a public authority has acted (or proposes to act) in a way which is made unlawful by section 6(1) may—

    (a) bring proceedings against the authority under this Act in the appropriate court or tribunal; or

    (b) rely on the Convention right or rights concerned in any legal proceedings,

but only if he is (or would be) a victim of the unlawful act.

(2) In subsection (1)(a) 'appropriate court or tribunal' means such court or tribunal as may be determined in accordance with rules; and proceedings against an authority include a counter claim or similar proceeding.

(3) If the proceedings are brought on an application for judicial review, the applicant is to be taken to have a sufficient interest in relation to the unlawful act only if he is, or would be, a victim of that act.

(4) If the proceedings are made by way of a petition for judicial review in Scotland, the applicant shall be taken to have title and interest to sue in relation to the unlawful act only if he is, or would be, a victim of that act.

(5) Proceedings under subsection (1)(a) must be brought before the end of—

    (a) the period of one year beginning with the date on which the act complained of took place; or

    (b) such longer period as the court or tribunal considers equitable having regard to all the circumstances,

but that is subject to any rule imposing a stricter time limit in relation to the procedure in question.

(6) In subsection (1)(b) 'legal proceedings' includes—

    (a) proceedings brought by or at the instigation of a public authority; and

    (b) an appeal against the decision of a court or tribunal.

(7) For the purposes of this section, a person is a victim of an unlawful act only if he would be a victim for the purposes of Article 34 of the Convention if proceedings were brought in the European Court of Human Rights in respect of that act.

(8) Nothing in this Act creates a criminal offence.

(9) In this section 'rules' means—

    (a) in relation to proceedings before a court or tribunal outside Scotland, rules made by the Lord Chancellor or the Secretary of State for the purposes of this section or rules of court,

    (b) in relation to proceedings before a court or tribunal in Scotland, rules made by the Secretary of State for those purposes,

    (c) in relation to proceedings before a tribunal in Northern Ireland—

    (i) which deals with transferred matters; and
    (ii) for which no rules made under paragraph (a) are in force,

    rules made by a Northern Ireland Department for those purposes,

and includes provision made by order under section 1 of the Courts and Legal Services Act 1990.

(10) In making rules, regard must be had to section 9.

(11) The Minister who has power to make rules in relation to a particular tribunal may, to the extent he considers it necessary to ensure the tribunal can provide an appropriate remedy in relation to an act (or proposed act) of a public authority which is (or would be) unlawful as a result of section 6(1), by order add to—

    (a) the relief or remedies which the tribunal may grant; or
    (b) the grounds on which it may grant any of them.

(12) An order made under subsection (11) may contain such incidental, supplemental, consequential or transitional provision as the Minister making it considers appropriate.

(13) 'The Minister' includes the Northern Ireland department concerned."

(2) Section 22 of the HRA:

"(4) Paragraph (b) of subsection (1) of section 7 applies to proceedings brought by or at the instigation of a public authority whenever the act in question took place; but otherwise that subsection does not apply to an act taking place before the coming into force of that section."

Key Principle: **A defendant whose trial took place before the coming into force of the HRA 1998 was not entitled to rely in an appeal on an alleged breach of his Convention rights under section 22(4) of the HRA.**

R. v. Lambert
For facts see p. 4.

Held: (HL) Since the relevant provisions of the HRA were not in force at the date of the trial, the decision of the court could not be challenged on the ground that it had acted in a manner contrary to the European Convention on Human Rights. The House should still however consider whether the transfer of the burden of proof under section 28 of the Misuse of Drugs Act 1971 was contrary to the Convention. [2001] 3 W.L.R. 206

R. v. Kansal (No. 2)

At his trial in 1992 for obtaining property by deception, the prosecution adduced against the defendant answers he had given under compulsion when he was examined under oath in bankruptcy proceedings. The trial judge admitted the answers despite a defence submission that it was unfair to do so. His appeal was dismissed on the basis that the Insolvency Act 1986 had abrogated his privilege against self-incrimination and made his answers admissible in any proceedings. In 2000 he appealed to the Court of Appeal which quashed his conviction on the basis that the 1998 Act had made the right to a fair trial retrospective. The Crown appealed.

Held: (HL) The House was bound by the decision of the majority in *R. v. Lambert* [2001] 3 W.L.R. 206, that appeals were excluded from the retrospectivity provisions of the 1998 Act. *Lambert* had been decided after the Court of Appeal decision in the appellant's case and the House would not depart from it without a compelling reason to do so. In tendering the disputed evidence, the prosecutor had been acting in accordance with primary legislation which could not at the time have been read differently in accordance with section 6 of the 1998 Act. Accordingly there had been no ground for the Court of Appeal to declare the conviction unsafe and the conviction would be reinstated. [2001] 3 W.L.R. 1562

Commentary

The Court of Appeal in *Lambert* had commented that judicial authorities were divided as to the retrospective nature of section 22(4) of the HRA. This states that the right to rely on Convention rights in section 7(1)(5) of the Act "applies to proceedings brought by or at the instigation of a public authority whenever the act in question took place". In the House of Lords, the majority (Lord Steyn dissenting) held that an appeal brought by an unsuccessful defendant was not to be treated as proceedings brought by a public authority. (Despite this finding the court did consider the substantive issue of the reverse onus of proof). Lord Steyn considered that if there has been a breach of the Convention, whenever it occurred, it must be wrong to uphold the conviction, due to the requirements in section 6 of the HRA. In *R. v. DPP, ex parte Kebilene* [2000] 2 A.C. 326 the majority had held that a criminal prosecution was "proceedings brought . . . by a public authority" (see also pp. 6, 80). In *R. (Mahmood) v. Secretary of State for the Home Department* [2001] 1 W.L.R. 840, an immigration decision case, the Court of Appeal stated that a court required to review an administrative decision made before the incorporation of the Convention was not obliged to consider Convention rights as having been incorporated into domestic law by the 1998 Act but that since the Secretary of State had stated that he had had regard to Article 8 of the Convention when giving his decision the court ought to approach the decision as if the 1998 Act had been in force.

Key Principle: **Evidence could not be excluded as being unfair when there had been lawful compliance with an Act of Parliament at the time of the trial.**

R. v. Lyons

The appellants were convicted in 1990 of dishonest conduct in the course of a takeover bid. The European Court of Human Rights held in 1996 that the use at the trial of transcripts of defendants' interviews under compulsion with Department of Trade inspectors violated their right to a fair trial. They sought to overturn their convictions relying on the HRA.

Held: (CA) The case was indistinguishable from *R. v. Kansal* (above), save that in *Kansal* there had been no finding by the European Court of Human Rights. The defendants could not rely on Article 46 of the E.C. Treaty, since that imposed no obligation on the state to reopen convictions. In any event the will of Parliament superseded any international obligation. It could not be said that the evidence should have been excluded as unfair when there had been lawful compliance with an Act of Parliament. Unfairness for the purposes of section 78 of the Police and Criminal Evidence Act 1984 could not arise merely from the use of compelled answers because parliament had expressly authorised their use. (2001) *The Times,* December 21

Commentary

In *Secretary of State for the Home Department v. Wainright,* (2002) *The Times,* January 4 the Court of Appeal held that the HRA could not change substantive law by introducing a retrospective right to privacy which did not exist at common law. (See Chapter 6).

___

Key Principle: **The requirement in section 3(1) of the HRA that so far as it is possible to do so legislation must be read and given effect to in a way compatible with Convention rights should be followed in all cases coming before the courts on or after October 2, 2000, irrespective of when the activities forming the subject matter of the cases took place.**

J A Pye (Oxford) Ltd v. Graham
The claimant sought possession of land from the defendants, who asserted adverse possession. The judge held that the defendants had the necessary intention to possess the disputed land, but expressed sympathy in his judgment with the view that this result did not accord with justice and involved a dispossession of property rights which was illogical, disproportionate and draconian. On appeal the claimant contended that the provisions of the Limitation Act 1980, which barred their claim to the land after 12 years adverse possession, should be interpreted in the light of section 3(1) of the HRA.

Held: (CA, *obiter*) Section 3(1) imposed a clear obligation on the courts in respect of their interpretation of legislation which applied irrespective of the date of the legislation. There was no reason to adopt one interpretation of a statute from October 2, 2000 onwards in a case involving activities before that date, and a different interpretation where the activities took place after that date. [2001] 2 W.L.R. 1293

Public Authorities

Key Principle: **Section 6 of the HRA—Acts of public authorities:**

"(1) It is unlawful for a public authority to act in a way which is incompatible with a Convention right.

(2) Subsection (1) does not apply to an act if—

    (a) as the result of one or more provisions of primary legislation, the authority could not have acted differently; or

(b) in the case of one or more provisions of, or made under, primary legislation which cannot be read or given effect in a way which is compatible with the Convention rights, the authority was acting so as to give effect to or enforce those provisions.

(3) In this section 'public authority' includes—

    (a) a court or tribunal, and

    (b) any person certain of whose functions are functions of a public nature,

but does not include either House of Parliament or a person exercising functions in connection with proceedings in Parliament.

(4) In subsection (3) 'Parliament' does not include the House of Lords in its judicial capacity.

(5) In relation to a particular act, a person is not a public authority by virtue only of subsection (3)(b) if the nature of the act is private.

(6) 'An act' includes a failure to act but does not include a failure to—

    (a) introduce in, or lay before, Parliament a proposal for legislation; or

    (b) make any primary legislation or remedial order."

Key Principle: **The Strasbourg jurisprudence may invoke proportionality as a new ground of judicial review.**

R. (Daly) v. Secretary of State for the Home Department
The applicant, a prisoner, had stored in his cell correspondence with his solicitor. He was, like all prisoners in a closed prison, subject to standard cell searching without him being present. The applicant sought leave for judicial review of the decision to require examination of prisoners' legally privileged correspondence in his absence.

Held: (HL) A person sentenced to custodial order retained the right to communicate confidentially with a legal adviser under the seal of legal professional privilege. The current policy amounted to an interference with the applicant's rights under

Article 8(1) to a greater extent than was necessary for the prevention of disorder and crime. The courts should adopt a test of proportionality in reviewing executive decisions. [2001] 2 A.C. 532

Commentary
In *R. v. Secretary of State for the Environment Transport and the Regions, ex parte Holding and Barnes and Others (Alconbury)* 2001 Lord Slynn stated (para. 51):

> "I consider that even without reference to the Human Rights Act the time has come to recognise that this principle [of proportionality] is part of English administrative laws, not only when judges are dealing with Community acts but also when they are dealing with acts subject to domestic law. Trying to keep the *Wednesbury* principle and proportionality in separate compartments seems to me to be unnecessary and confusing."

Lord Steyn here indicated that the "heightened scrutiny test" which was developed for human rights inferences in *R. v. Ministry of Defence, ex parte Smith* [1996] Q.B. 517 1995 may not necessarily be appropriate. (See p. 104). The Strasbourg Court stated that the threshold at which the Court of Appeal could find the MoD policy irrational was "placed so high that it effectively excluded any consideration by the domestic courts of the question of whether the interference with the applicants' rights answered a pressing social need or was proportionate to the national security and public order aims pursued, principles which lie at the heart of the Court's analysis of complaints under Article 8 of the Convention". This test was applied in *Daly*, signalling in effect that proportionality is a new ground of review. Lord Steyn denied that this meant a shift to review on merits. The House of Lords declared in this case that it was following *Campbell v. U.K.* (1993) 15 E.H.R.R. 137 as well as a number of English authorities including *R. v. Secretary of State for the Home Department ex parte Leech* [1994] Q.B. 198. The effect of sections 2 and 3 of the HRA will be that the Strasbourg method of judicial reasoning will have increasing impact in English courts. However, it should be noted that the duty is to take account of the Strasbourg case law, not necessarily to follow it. It may be that the English courts will surpass the Strasbourg jurisprudence in developing concepts of rights. One example of this is the House of Lords decision in *Fitzpatrick v. Sterling Housing Association* [1999] 3 W.L.R. 1113 where it found as a matter of English law that a stable gay relationship was a family, thus enabling the surviving partner of a homosexual to retain a lease on a council flat. This was despite the fact that Strasbourg had not hitherto accepted that gay relationships were the basis of a family.

Key Principle: **Private bodies to which public authorities had delegated some of their functions might not be held accountable in public law.**

Donoghue v. Poplar Housing and Regeneration Community Association Ltd

The appellant had been originally granted a tenancy by the local authority which later transferred it to Poplar Housing and Regeneration Community Association Ltd (Poplar). Poplar was a non-profit organisation created by the local authority to manage the housing stock. An order was made by the local authority for the possession of the appellant's property which was held under an assumed shorthold tenancy according to section 21 of the Housing Act 1988. The authority had determined that the appellant was intentionally homeless. The appellant appealed against the order for possession on the grounds that Poplar, being a public authority in terms of section 6 of the HRA was making a disproportionate interference under Article 8 right to respect for private life. A subsidiary issue was the procedure to be followed when the crown was notified that the court might be considering a declaration of incompatibility under section 4 of the HRA.

Held: (CA) Poplar was a public authority but there was no breach of Article 8. The transfer by the local authority to Poplar of their housing stock did not also transfer their public duties but only the means by which to enact them. Providing houses for rent was not a public duty. The court should defer to the will of Parliament which had given the courts limited intervention in the area of possession against people with low housing priority. (2001) U.K.H.R.R. 693

Commentary

The court gave extensive consideration to the factors which should be taken into account in deciding whether a body is a public authority. Many of these were derived from the pre-existing administrative law jurisprudence but some controversial new issues were raised. In *Costello-Roberts v. U.K.* (1995) 19 E.H.R.R. 112 the Strasbourg Court stated that "the state cannot absolve itself from responsibility by delegating its obligations to private bodies or individuals". (See also pp. 53, 120). However in *Donoghue* the Court of Appeal expressed the view that a local authority in privatising some functions would not automatically make the actions of the private company public in nature. More controversially it stated that providing houses for rent was not in itself a public duty, no matter which section of society the houses were for. (see also the Court of Appeal decision in *St Brice v. Southwark LBC, The Times*, August 6, 2001. In addition the fact that Poplar was a charity meant that the motivation of the organisation was more likely to be in the public good but that was not an indicator that it was a public body in terms of section 4 of the HRA. In the instant case Poplar was functioning as a public authority. In *Heather v. The Leonard Cheshire Foundation* [2001] EWHC Admin 429 the Administrative Court found that the charity was not to be amenable to judicial review despite the fact that many local authorities used it to provide care and support services for the disabled. In *RSPCA v. HM Attorney-General* [2001] 3 All E.R. 530 the court found that the RSPCA was not a public authority for the purposes of the 1998 Act. Some commentators have pointed out that there are advantages in excluding a body from the designation of "public authority" since as a result it has potential standing as a victim to make a claim under the Act in appropriate circumstances. Professor Dawn Oliver for example argues that the interpretation of "public authority" under the Act should be restrictive. If this were not so a whole range of institutions which might wish to make claims under the Act would not be able to do so. She gives the universities, charities and the BBC as examples and expresses concern lest the Government restricted research, broadcasting and charitable campaigning without fear of counter challenge under Article 10 of ECHR. This line of argument suggests that amenability to judicial review should not necessarily be the determining factor in deciding whether a body was a "public authority" for the purposes of the HRA. Oliver comments, "the issues are different [in human rights cases] and in particular there is no reason why bodies which violate Convention rights when exercising public functions should benefit from the protection of Order 53, the existence of which may have influenced the

court in developing the concept of public function for the pur-
poses of that jurisdiction" ("The Frontiers of the State: Public
Authorities and Public Functions under the Human Rights Act"
(Autumn 2001) *Public Law* at 476).

Key Principle: **Public authorities may have liabilities under
the HRA some of which are also available under the common
law or statute.**

Marcic v. Thames Water Utilities

The complainant's house was subject to persistent flooding
because of a back flow from a defective sewer. The defendant
statutory authority had refused to remedy the cause.

Held: (CA) A sewerage undertaker was liable in nuisance at
common law for failing to take steps to remedy a nuisance
caused by the discharge of sewerage onto the claimant's land.
The defendants had inherited a system of drainage which was
inadequate to meet the demands put on it by third parties
discharging sewage by right. The defendant was in no better
position than a landowner on whose property a hazard had
naturally accumulated. On the facts following the decision in
Leakey v. National Trust [1980] 1 Q.B. 485 the defendant was
obliged to take reasonable steps to prevent discharge of sewage
onto the claimant's property. The defendant was a large undertaker which could not reasonably claim lack of resources as a
reason for doing nothing to prevent the flooding of the claimant's property. The defendant had infringed the claimant's
rights under Article 8 and Article 1 of the First Protocol to the
European Convention on Human Rights. *The Times*, February
14, 2002

Commentary

In giving his decision at first instance, Judge Richard Havery said:
"In the absence of authority I would have thought that [Article 8
and Protocol 1, Article 1] had nothing to do with the case. I would
have been wrong." Havery's decision was hailed as creating a new
constitutional tort under the HRA. But the Court of Appeal was
anxious to bring the decision within the existing common law
framework.

3. KILLING, TORTURE, SLAVERY

Right to life

Key Principle: **Article 2 of the ECHR—Right to life:**

"1 Everyone's right to life shall be protected by law. No one shall be deprived of his life intentionally save in the execution of a sentence of a court following his conviction of a crime for which this penalty is provided by law.

2 Deprivation of life shall not be regarded as inflicted in contravention of this article when it results from the use of force which is no more than absolutely necessary:

    a in defence of any person from unlawful violence;
    b in order to effect a lawful arrest or to prevent the escape of a person lawfully detained;
    c in action lawfully taken for the purpose of quelling a riot or insurrection."

Key Principle: **Article 2 of the ECHR is not concerned solely with intentional killing but also covers situations where the unintended outcome of the state's actions is the deprivation of life.**

Association X v. U.K.
The Government had instituted a voluntary scheme for vaccination of children. Some of the children had suffered injury or died. The Association of parents of these children complained that the scheme was poorly administered and that proper steps had not been taken to avoid the risk of serious injury or death.

Held: (Commission) On the facts there was no violation since "there exists a general common knowledge that vaccination schemes involve certain risks". The state had established a system for control and supervision which was "sufficient to comply with obligation to protect life under Article 2 of the Convention". (1978) 14 D.R. 31

Commentary
It is implicit in the Commission's findings that without a proper system of control and supervision there might have been a breach of Article 2. It is also clear that the state is permitted to introduce measures involving medical risks to individuals but which are for the general good.

Key Principle: **The scope of Article 2 does not cover prescribing how resources in a national health service should be allocated.**

Taylor v. U.K.
Parents whose children had been unlawfully killed or injured in hospital by nurse Beverley Allitt in violation of Article 2. Allitt was convicted of murder of four children, the attempted murder of three children and of causing grievous bodily harm to six children. The parents had pressed for a public inquiry into the tragedy but only an internal inquiry was held. The parents argued that financial and other shortcomings of the National Health Service had allowed an untrained and dangerous person to care for their children unsupervised. The internal inquiry report did not comment directly on the parents' claims that the hospital had been poorly funded and understaffed. The parents claimed on their own behalf and on that of their children. They alleged that they continued to be affected by the events which had arisen from government failings and which could be repeated in the future.

Held: (Commission) The organisation and the funding of the National Health service does not fall within the scope of Article 2. "Any doubts which may consequently arise as to the policies adopted in the field of public health are, in the Commission's opinion, matters for public and political debate which fall outside the scope of Article 2 and the other provisions of the Convention." [1994] 79–A D.R. 127

Commentary
This case leaves unanswered the question of how far the state has a positive duty to provide resources to preserve life. It is a par-

ticularly pertinent issue in relation to the state's responsibility to provide life-saving medical treatment. In *R. v. Cambridgeshire Health Authority, ex parte B* [1995] 1 F.L.R. 1055 the Court of Appeal overturning the decision of the High Court held that the Health Authority was entitled to refuse to fund potential life-saving treatment for a young child since it was entitled to deploy its resources as best it could. It seems in the light of *Taylor v. U.K.* that such a decision would not necessarily be resisted in the light of the HRA. However, it should be noted that Article 14 requires public authorities to safeguard Convention rights without discrimination on any ground. It might therefore be the case that if life saving treatment was withheld on the grounds of age, or youth or mental condition that such action was a breach of Article 14 taken together with Article 2.

Reasonableness Test

Key Principle: **The state's positive duty to protect life must be construed in the light of prevailing circumstances.**

Osman v. U.K.
A teacher harassed and intimidated a pupil and his family. He eventually killed the pupil. The family argued that the police, who had been alerted to the situation, had not taken sufficient measures to protect the family.

Held: (ECtHR) There was no violation of Article 2 since none of the events leading up to the killing had appeared to be threatening the life of the boy. The court considered however that in order for there to be a breach of Article 2 it was not necessary to demonstrate that there had been "gross negligence or wilful disregard of the duty to protect life". It was "sufficient for an applicant to show that the authorities did not do all that could reasonably be expected of them to avoid a real and immediate risk to life of which they have or ought to have knowledge." It was also necessary on the other hand to ensure that the police acted in a way which respected due process and the guarantees in Articles 5 and 8. [1999] 1 F.L.R. 193 (See also p. 17).

Keenan v. U.K. 2001
A mentally ill person committed suicide. The family argued that there was a violation of Article 2 in that the authorities had not taken sufficient care.

Held: (ECtHR) There was no violation of Article 2 since the prison authorities made a reasonable response to his conduct and had not omitted any step which should reasonably have been taken. (App. No. 27229/95) [2001] H.R. 178

Commentary
In *Guerra v. Italy* (1998) 26 E.H.R.R. 357 the court also held that the authorities only had an obligation to inform local people about environmental dangers which posed a potential threat to health in "circumstances which forseeably and on substantial grounds present a real risk of danger": that was not so in that case. However, although the authorities might be able to argue in defence of an act under Article 2 that they had acted reasonably, the content of "reasonableness" is open to various interpretations. The common law has accepted the justification of the interests of the patient for the decision of doctors to turn off the life-support system of someone who is in a permanent vegetative state. In *Airedale NHS Trust v. Bland* [1993] A.C. 789 Lord Mustill had considered on additional argument based on the best interests of the community as a whole. However although this was persuasive "in social terms" he did not consider that the House of Lords was qualified to make such an assessment.

Key Principle: **The obligation of a public authority under Article 2 may be to avoid making a decision exposing anyone to the real possibility of a risk to life in the future.**

R. v. Lord Saville, ex parte (1) 28 Widgery Soldiers (2) 8 Inquiry Soldiers
This was a challenge by way of judicial review of a decision made by the Bloody Sunday Inquiry Tribunal which ruled that soldier witnesses who are to give oral evidence before the Tribunal over a period of six months should do so in the Londonderry Guildhall, where the Tribunal had for the most part sat, rather than in London or in some other part of Great Britain. The soldier witnesses who were due to give evidence

claimed that they would be exposed to lethal danger. The tribunal ruled that they must nevertheless give evidence. They appealed first to the Divisional Court by way of judicial review and then to the Court of Appeal. It was common ground that the High Court had a reviewing jurisdiction in relation to decisions of the Tribunal but it was argued that the Tribunal did not fall within the ambit of section 6 of the HRA and so the HRA did not apply.

Held: (CA) The Tribunal has to comply with the HRA and so the High Court had jurisdiction to entertain the application. The Tribunal had misdirected itself in law by applying the wrong test when assessing the risk to the lives of the soldiers if they gave evidence in Londonderry. It was not open to the Tribunal to conclude that the soldiers had no reasonable fears for their own safety. The test of "real and immediate" danger to life was not the appropriate test to invoke in the present circumstances. The appropriate course was to consider the nature of the witnesses' fears, the extent to which they were objectively founded and then to consider the extent to which those fears would be reduced if the soldiers' evidence were taken elsewhere in the United Kingdom. That had to be balanced against the adverse consequences to the inquiry of taking the evidence outside Londonderry. The risk posed in Londonderry to the soldier witnesses was real and fairness required that their evidence be taken elsewhere. The Administrative Court was correct in concluding that the Bloody Sunday Inquiry's ruling on the venue of soldier—witness hearings did not comply with the requirements of Article 2. *Times Law Reports*, December 21, 2001

Commentary

The Administrative court compared the tests set out on the one hand in *Osman* (see above) and on the other in *R. v. Governor of Pentonville Prison, ex parte Fernandez* (1971) 1 W.L.R. 987 and *R. v. Lord Saville and Another, ex parte A* (1999) 4 All E.R. 860. These tests were different. In *Osman* the European Court of Human Rights had limited the obligation of the state to intervene to protect against the activities of third parties in circumstances in which there is a real and immediate risk to life. It should have considered the tests in *ex parte Fernandez* and *ex parte A* where the obligation of a public authority was defined more broadly. The degree of risk set out in *Osman* was well above the threshold that would engage Article 2.

Absolutely Necessary Force

Key Principle: **Deprivation of life is not inflicted in contravention of Article 2 when it results from the use of force which is no more than absolutely necessary (1) in defence of any person from unlawful violence or (2) in order to effect a lawful arrest or to prevent the escape of a person lawfully detained or (3) action lawfully taken for the purpose of quelling a riot or insurrection.**

McCann v. U.K. 1994
Three Provisional IRA members were in Gibraltar to plant a car bomb. At the time, however, there was no bomb in Gibraltar; it was in fact in a long stay facility in Spain. Soldiers of the Special Air Service shot the three IRA members dead in the street. The soldiers claimed in each case that they had opened fire because they suspected that their targets were about to set off a bomb by remote control. A coroner's jury in Gibraltar found the killings lawful. Attempts by the families of the dead men to bring judicial review proceedings failed.

Held: (ECtHR) In assessing whether the use of force had been "absolutely necessary", the court must subject the deprivation of life to the most careful scrutiny and take into account not only the actions of the state agents who used the force, but also all the surrounding circumstances. The test of "absolutely necessary" requires that "a stricter and more compelling test of necessity must be employed from that normally applicable when determining whether the state's action is 'necessary in a democratic society'". There was no violation of Article 2 in the actions of the soldiers who shot the terrorists but there was a violation as regards the control and organisation of the operation. The court refused to award damages, however, accepting that the men had been intending to plant a bomb. (1996) 21 E.H.R.R. 97

Stewart v. U.K. 1984
The applicant's son, a 13 year old boy, was killed by a soldier in Northern Ireland firing a plastic bullet into a rioting crowd. She had taken an unsuccessful case as administratrix of the child for assault, battery and trespass to the person. The appeal judge in

the hearing had found that the firing was a reasonable and lawful use of force for the prevention of crime since the boy had been participating in a riot. The applicant claimed a violation of Article 2.

Held: (Commission) There was no violation of Article 2. Force was "absolutely necessary" if it was "strictly proportionate to the achievement of the permitted purpose". The court considered that Article 2(2) did cover unintentional as well as intentional killings. (1984) 39 D.R. 162

Commentary
The test of absolute necessity applied by the Court and the Commission imposes a higher standard than that under English statutory law. A subjective test of reasonableness is applied in the Criminal Law Act 1967, s. 3. The case illustrates that the Court and Commission will take into account exceptional circumstances such as that in Northern Ireland which face states.

Investigation of Deaths

Key Principle: **Article 2 requires a proper investigation of suspicious deaths.**

Jordan v. U.K.
Relatives of people killed by the security services in Northern Ireland complained that their right to life had been violated by the authorities' failure to conduct a proper investigation into the circumstances of their deaths. They also, in two of the cases, alleged violation of the right to a fair trial, and in all four cases discrimination and a breach of the right to an effective remedy.

Held: (ECtHR) Article 2 ranked as one of the most fundamental provisions in the Convention, and no derogation was permitted in peacetime. The circumstances in which deprivation of a life could be justified had to be strictly construed. The burden of proof rested on the authorities to provide a satisfactory and convincing explanation of the deaths or of persons or within their control in custody. The Article covered not only intentional killing but also all situations where it was permitted to use force which could result, as an unintended outcome, in the deprivation of life. It required by implication some form of effective official investigation on the authorities' own motion. In all cases the next of kin of the victim had to be involved in the procedure to the extent necessary to safeguard his or her legitimate interests. The court rejected the applicants' other complaints. (App. Nos 24746/94, 28883/95, 37715/97) [2001] H.R. 178

R. (Middleton) v. HM Coroner for Western Somersetshire

Colin Middleton had died while in prison serving a life sentence. His mother contended that the present conduct of inquests was not compatible with Article 2. It was argued that in cases where it is alleged that the deceased died while in custody as a result of negligence by officers of the State the holding of an inquest did not satisfy the obligations of the state because of restrictions on the permissible findings of the inquest.

Held: (QBD) The unavailability of a verdict of neglect in a case like this did not necessarily mean that an inquest did not satisfy the procedural requirements of Article 2. However where the neglect of state officials was a substantial contributory cause of death it was necessary to have a formal finding as such. It was important that failings by the state should be open to public investigation and as a result an inquest would not necessarily satisfy the procedural requirements of the ECHR. However on the facts a further investigation was not appropriate since it would cause more stress to the family. [2001] EWHC Admin 1043

Commentary

The procedure for inquest, police investigation and the role of the Police Complaints Authority may now come under scrutiny as a result of these cases. In *Taylor v. U.K.* the parents failed in a claim that the refusal to establish a public inquiry breached Article 2. (See p. 34)

Abortion

Key Principle: **Article 2 could restrict the availability of an abortion but national authorities enjoy a wide margin of appreciation and recognising the absolute right to life of a foetus would be contrary to the object and purpose of the Convention.**

Paton v. U.K.

A husband living separately from his wife, tried to stop her having an abortion. The operation was carried out under legislation which permitted abortions after ten weeks to avert the risk of injury to the physical or mental health of the pregnant woman.

Held: (Commission) Case inadmissible. Article 2 does not require states to put a complete ban on abortions since a foetus has no "absolute right to life". "The life of the foetus is intimately connected with and cannot be regarded in isolation of the pregnant woman. If Article 2 were held to cover the foetus and its protection under the Article were, in the absence of any express limitation, seen as absolute, as abortion would have to be considered as prohibited even where the continuance of the pregnancy would involve a serious risk to the life of the pregnant woman". The Commission held this outcome as unacceptable since it would mean that the "unborn life" of the foetus would be taken to have a higher value than the life of the pregnant woman. The Commission observed that there were two other possible interpretations of Article 2 namely that the foetus had no right to life or that any right it did have was subject to limitations. Since in this case even if the second interpretation was accepted there was no breach of Article 2, the Commission did not see the need to pronounce which of the two interpretations was correct. (1980) 19 D.R. 244

Commentary

This case concerned the abortion of a foetus of under 10 weeks. At that stage viable life outside the mother is impossible. Although not excluding the possibility that under certain circumstances Article 2 does protect the foetus, the Commission was silent on what those circumstances were. In *Open Door Counselling and Dublin Well Woman v. Ireland* (1993) 15 E.H.R.R. 244 the Court held that injunctions preventing women from leafleting in favour of abortion were disproportionate and therefore there were violations of Article 10. This case thus concerned the applicants' rights to disseminate information about abortion rather than the right to abortion. However, the Court did state that Article 2 could in principle restrict the availability of abortion while acknowledging that "National authorities enjoy a wide margin of appreciation in matters of morals, particularly in an area such as the present which touches on matters of belief concerning the nature of human life." It also stated that Article 10 should not be interpreted in such a way as to limit the right to life. Note that Article 2 does not declare that life starts at conception in contrast with Article 4 of the American Convention on Human Rights. Abortion may also raise rights of the parents under Article 8 (see below).

No Right to Assisted Suicide

Key Principle: **Section 21(1) of the Suicide Act 1961 was not incompatible with the European Convention on Human Rights.**

Pretty v. DPP
P was terminally ill with motor neurone disease. She wished to take her own life but her physical incapacity meant she required assistance to commit suicide. Section 21(1) of the Suicide Act 1961 made it a criminal offence for a person to assist the suicide of another. Section 2(4) of the Act provided that no proceedings for that offence could be instituted except by or with the consent of the Director of Public Prosecutions (DPP). P appealed from a decision of the Divisional Court that the DPP had correctly refused to undertake not to prosecute P's husband if he were to assist his wife to commit suicide. She submitted that Article 2 of the European Convention on Human Rights when read in conjunction with Protocol 6 Article 1 and Protocol 6 Article 2 of the Convention guaranteed that an individual could choose whether or not to live. She also submitted that the DPP's refusal subjected her to inhuman or degrading treatment in breach of Article 3 of the ECHR.

Held: (HL) (1) Article 2 did not confer a negative right to end life; (2) there was no common law right to take a life; (3) P had the burden of proof to establish the DPP's decision breached the ECHR; (4) Articles 2 and 3 were complementary and there was nothing in Article 3 that affected an individual's right to choose not to live; (5) Rights under Article 8, 9 or 14 were not infringed; the 1961 Act did not confer a right to commit suicide, it merely abrogated the rule of law that it was a crime. [2001] UKHL 61

Commentary
The House drew on Convention and common law principles in making its judgment. At common law someone else cannot take a

person's life (see *Airedale NHS Trust v. Bland* [1993] A.C. 789)
nor could fatality be a primary aim of treatment (see *Re J (a minor)
(wardship: medical treatment)* [1991] Fam. 33. The House considered that the most detailed and erudite discussion of the issues
raised by the appeal was to be found in the Canadian case
Rodriguez v. Attorney-General of Canada (1994) 2 L.R.C. 136. The
applicant also alleged breaches of Articles 8, 9 and 14 and that the
United Kingdom's blanket refusal to allow assistance with suicides
was disproportionate in view of P being in full command of her
mental faculties, the absence of harm to anyone else, the immi-
nence of her death and her willingness to commit suicide herself
were she able to. The House found no breaches of those articles.
In *Widmer v. Switzerland* (1993, unreported) the Commission held
that Article 2 does not require states to make passive euthanasia a
crime.

Key Principle: **Article 3 of the ECHR—Prohibition of torture:
"No one shall be subjected to torture or to inhuman or
degrading treatment or punishment."**

Key Principle: **Article 3 covers three levels of conduct defined
as:**

"a Torture: deliberate inhuman treatment causing very serious and cruel suffering.

b Inhuman treatment or punishment: the infliction of
   intense physical and mental suffering.

c Degrading treatment: Ill treatment designed to arouse in
   victims feelings of fear, anguish and inferiority capable of
   humiliating and debasing them and possibly breaking
   their physical and moral resistance."

Ireland v. U.K. 1978
Detainees in Northern Ireland were obliged to stand against a
wall for hours in extremely uncomfortable positions. They were
interrogated wearing dark hoods and deprived of sleep and
adequate food and drink. They were also subjected to noise.

Held: (ECtHR) The court disagreed with the Commission's findings that these techniques amounted to torture. They did however constitute inhuman and degrading treatment. The court listed the factors to take into account. These included sex, age and the state of health of the victim. It stated that the authority's activities should reach a minimum level of severity to bring them within the Article. "Degrading" did not mean simply disagreeable or uncomfortable. Actions in private as well as in front of others could fall within the Article. (1978) 2 E.H.R.R. 25

Key Principle: **Torture can consist of the imposition of mental suffering.**

Denmark v. Greece (The Greek Case)

Prisoners in Athen's jails were subjected to severe overcrowding in cells and corridors with little natural light, were given no beds or mattresses. They were refused or had access delayed to medical treatment. They were also physically ill-treated.

Held: (Commission) The treatment amounted to torture in that it included "the infliction of mental suffering by creating a state of anguish and stress by means other than bodily assault. The Commission's finding of torture was confirmed by the Council of Ministers. The Commission stated that "mental suffering leading to acute psychiatric disturbances falls into the category of treatment prohibited by Article 3 of the Convention". (1969) 12 YB Spec. Vol.

Commentary

This is one of the few cases where a state has taken action against another state. The Commission found that slaps or blows to the head might not breach Article 3 but this position has been changed somewhat in subsequent case law see for example *Tomasi v. France* (1993) 15 E.H.R.R. 1. The Commission's finding was upheld by the Committee of Ministers. For another acknowledgement that mental anguish can constitute torture see also *Ireland v. U.K.* (1978) 2 E.H.R.R. 25.

Key Principle: **States have a positive obligation to prevent torture.**

Chahal v. U.K.
The applicant was faced with deportation to India because his presence in the United Kingdom was considered not conducive to the public good on the grounds of national security. He had been denied asylum. He claimed that there was a violation of Article 3 since his deportation would expose him to a real risk he would be tortured in India.

Held: (ECtHR) Despite the difficulties faced by states in protecting their citizens from terrorist violence "the Convention prohibits in absolute terms torture or inhuman or degrading treatment or punishment, irrespective of the victim's conduct." There was therefore a violation of Article 3. (1997) 23 E.H.R.R. 413

Commentary
This case emphasises the absolute nature of the prohibitions in Article 3. However undesirable or dangerous the activities of the individual in question they cannot be a material consideration. There was also a violation in *D v. U.K.* (1997) 24 E.H.R.R. 423 where the person threatened with deportation had AIDS. He would have neither emotional nor financial support in the receiving country where there was a poor quality of medical care. The absolute prohibition contained in Article 3 should be respected whether or not the applicant had been given leave to enter the United Kingdom.

Key Principle: **Torture may arise where the threatened treatment is lawful.**

Soering v. U.K.
A German national faced extradition from Britain to face capital charges in the United States. He was in a prison hospital due to his dread of violence and homosexual abuse from other inmates. He claimed violations of Article 3 in that both the death penalty itself and waiting on "death row" for execution in the United States amounted to inhuman and degrading treatment.

Held: (ECtHR) The death penalty in itself was not an inhuman and degrading punishment within the meaning of Article 3. Article 3 did not in itself prohibit the death penalty since that would have nullified one of the exceptions to the right to life under Article 2(1). The court acknowledged that many Contracting States had abolished the death penalty which might be taken to abrogate the exception under Article 2(1). However the specific provision in the Sixth Protocol for the abolition of the death penalty was an indication that Article 3 could not have the meaning the application argued. There was nonetheless a violation of Article 3. Although the death penalty in the United States was not in itself illegal, the fact that the applicant might well be held for years on death row pending execution was a violation for which the United Kingdom would be responsible if the extradition went ahead. Extradition to non-Contracting States may give rise to a positive obligation under Article 3 if there is a real risk of torture or inhuman or degrading treatment or punishment in the requesting country. (1989) 11 E.H.R.R. 439

Commentary
The court stated that despite its decision in this case the circumstances of the death penalty could in principle give rise to an application under Article 3. A relevant factor would be changing attitudes in the Contracting States to executions. The Court referred to the United Nations Convention for the Prevention of Torture and Other Cruel, Inhuman or Degrading Treatment or Punishment and in particular Article 3 which states that "No State Party shall . . . extradite a person . . . where there are substantial grounds for believing that he would be in danger of being subjected to torture" and that it would be compatible with the values of the Convention that such an obligation existed. Protocol 6 Article 1 of the ECHR provides: "The death penalty shall be abolished. No one shall be condemned to such penalty or executed." It is a matter of some controversy whether the judicial Committee of the Privy Council which sits as the final court of appeal for certain former colonial countries will be bound by Protocol 6 in their decisions in death penalty cases. In ratifying Protocol 6 the United Kingdom only extended it expressly to Jersey, Guernsey and the Channel Islands. Article 56 of the European Convention on Human Rights, which was not included in the HRA, allows the state to extend the provisions of the Convention to "all or any territory for whose international relations it is responsible". This has not included the Caribbean. However the Privy Council in considering appeals involving the

death penalty has drawn on case law from international and European Convention organs. (See *Pratt v. Attorney-General for Jamaica* [1993] 3 W.L.R. 995).

Responsibility for Torture

Key Principle: **Former heads of state do not have immunity in respect of acts of torture committed while head of state contrary to the 1984 International Convention Against Torture.**

R. v. Bow Street Metropolitan Stipendiary Magistrate ex parte Pinochet Ugarte (No. 3)

The former Chilean dictator was arrested in London on a Spanish warrant. The warrant alleged that he had ordered torture and hostage-taking while he was in power. The Divisional Court held that the applicant as a former head of state was entitled to immunity from civil and criminal process in the English courts in respect of acts committed in the exercise of sovereign power. The House of Lords allowed an appeal by the prosecutor, but this decision was set aside because one of the judges, Lord Hoffman, was an office-holder in a charity controlled by Amnesty International. The case was reheard before a differently constituted court.

Held: (HL) Though a former head of state had immunity from the criminal jurisdiction of the United Kingdom for acts done in his official capacity as head of state, torture was an international crime against humanity and there was a universal jurisdiction to extradite or punish a public official for torture. That principle extended to heads of state because the state parties who had created the international jurisdiction by the International Convention against Torture could not have intended to create an immunity for a head of state who was a torturer. [1999] 2 W.L.R. 827

Commentary

Two of their Lordships, Lords Millett and Phillips, stated that the systematic use of torture was an international crime for which there could be no immunity even before the United Nations Convention against Torture came into effect and consequently there was no immunity under customary international law for the offences relating to torture alleged against the applicant. This decision shows that English courts are prepared to apply customary international human rights law. Pinochet subsequently avoided extradition by pleading ill-health.

Key Principle: **The state may be responsible for the acts of its agents even when they are acting in breach of orders.**

Cyprus v. Turkey
The Cypriot Government claimed that the Turkish Government held responsibility for outrages on detainees including rapes.

Held: (Commission) The Commission accepted the allegations that a number of detainees had suffered rapes by Turkish soldiers and in two cases by Turkish officers and that the Turkish authorities had not taken sufficient measures to prevent this. (1982) 4 E.H.R.R. 482

Commentary
This case illustrates that the principle of strict liability applies to Article 3 since "It has not been shown that the Turkish authorities took adequate measures to prevent this happening or that they generally took any disciplinary measures following such incidents. The Commission therefore considers that the non prevention of the said acts is imputable to Turkey under the Convention." This approach was also evident in *Ireland v. U.K.* (see above) where the court held that the higher authorities of the state "are strictly liable for the conduct of their subordinates; they are under a duty to impose their will on subordinates and cannot shelter behind their inability to ensure that it is respected".

Prison conditions

Key Principle: **In the context or the treatment of prisoners the treatment must go beyond the usual element of humiliation associated with imprisonment after a criminal conviction in order to be a violation of Article 3.**

Tyrer v. U.K.
For facts and holding see pp. 7–8.

Commentary
The court made it clear that in order to cross the minimum threshold regard will be taken of all the circumstances of the case which include "the nature and context of the punishment itself and the manner and method of its execution". The personal characteristics of the victim are relevant including age, gender and state of health.

Key Principle: **The fact that the person concerned has brought the treatment on himself may be a relevant consideration in assessing whether a violation of the Article has occurred.**

McFeeley v. U.K. 1981
IRA prisoners had as a protest against their prison status smeared their cells with food and excrement. They claimed that their continued detention in the cells was inhuman and degrading treatment.

Held: (Commission) The self imposed condition of the cells could relieve the state from its responsibilities for the welfare of prisoners. The state had an obligation to keep the situation under constant review. There was no violation of Article 3. (1984) 38 D. & R. 11

Commentary
The Commission also found that there was nothing inherently degrading or objectionable about the requirement to wear prison uniform or to be subjected to intimate body searches. The Commission also considered that the object of achieving political prisoner status was not supported by international law. In other cases the Commission stated that the fact that a person has brought the treatment on himself cannot in itself absolve the state of its obligations under Article 3. Although such cases show the Commission has not absolved the state of all responsibility for self-inflicted harm under Article 3, it has in fact not found any violations. In *Hilton v. U.K.* (1981) 3 E.H.R.R. 104 the self-inflicted conditions were a result of an innate characteristic of the prisoner, namely his stressful personality which meant that he was incapable of accepting imprisonment. His distrust of fellow prisoners and warders led to his total isolation and his reduction to an

animal like state. The majority view of the Commission was that although it was critical of many of the measures taken by the authorities some of them were positive and there was no violation of Article 3. However the strong dissenting view of four commissioners was that the state's responsibility was engaged.

Key Principle: **A degrading punishment does not lose its degrading character just because it is believed to be or actually is an effective deterrent to or aid to maintain discipline.**

Tyrer v. U.K.
See p. 7.

Commentary
The Government sought to rely on what was then Article 63(3) of the Convention, now Article 56(3). This allows a state to extend the Convention to territories for whose international relations it is responsible. However the provisions should be applied with due regard to "local requirements". The Government argued that public opinion in the Isle of Man supported birching, making it it a "local requirement". However the court considered that there would have to be positive and conclusive proof of a requirement and beliefs and local opinion on their own were not sufficient.

Key Principle: **Lack of adequate specialist medical supervision of a known suicide risk prisoner violated Article 3.**

Keenan v. United Kingdom
The son of the applicant had died in Exeter Prison from asphyxia caused by self suspension. His medical history included symptoms of paranoia, aggression, violence and deliberate self harm.

Held: (ECtHR) The lack of effective monitoring of Mark Keenan's condition and the lack of informed psychiatric input into his assessment and treatment disclosed defects in the medical care provided to a mentally ill person known to be a suicide risk. In these circumstances the imposition of additional disciplinary punishment was not compatible with the standard of treatment required in respect of a mentally ill person. There was therefore a breach of Article 3. (App. No. 27229/95), April 3, 2001

Commentary
The court rejected the application to find a violation of Article 2. It was not apparent that the authorities omitted any step which should have reasonably been taken. Other cases have underlined that conditions of incarceration have to be very poor to engage Article 3. In *Delazarus v. U.K.* (1993) (App. No. 17525/90) February 16, a prisoner was segregated for over four months as a disciplinary measure. He was not allowed to communicate or associate with other prisoners and was locked in a cockroach infested cell for 23 hours a day with two half hour breaks in a pen the size of a tennis court. The application was held inadmissible.

Racial Discrimination

Key Principle: **Racial discrimination may amount to degrading treatment.**

East African Asians v. U.K.
The applicants were citizens of the United Kingdom and colonies and husbands of Commonwealth citizens who were already resident in the United Kingdom. The authorities refused them admission into the United Kingdom. The legislation however would have permitted wives to come into the United Kingdom to join their husbands. The Commission was asked to decide whether the discriminatory effect of the legislation applicable at the time could be regarded as degrading treatment under Article 3 on the grounds that "to single out a group of persons for different treatment on the basis of race may constitute a special form of affront to human dignity and might therefore be capable of constituting degrading treatment".

Held: (Commission) In relation to one group the Commission considered that "the racial discrimination to which the applicants have been publicly subjected by the . . . immigration legislation, constitutes an interference with their human dignity which amounted to . . . degrading treatment in the sense of Article 3 of the Convention". This group had been promised free entry to the United Kingdom and their continued residence in East Africa was illegal and they were stateless. With regard to the group of "protected persons" who were not British subjects since here the legislation did not distinguish between categories of persons on any racial basis there was no violation of Article 3. (1981) 3 E.H.R.R. 76

Commentary
The use of immigration controls is not in itself a violation of the ECHR. but controls based on racial discrimination could as here amount to degrading treatment. (See also p. 182).

Key Principle: **For there to be a violation of Article 3 it is not necessarily required required that the state should positively intend to degrade someone.**

Price v. U.K.
The applicant, a victim of the drug Thalidomide, was four limbed deficient. She was sentenced to seven days jail for refusing, in a judgment debt hearing, to answer questions on her financial position. She alleged that her committal and her treatment in prison violated Article 3. She had particular difficulty over reaching the bed and toilet, hygiene and fluid intake and mobility.

Held: (ECtHR) There was no evidence of any positive intention to humiliate or debase the applicant. However it constituted degrading treatment under Article 3 to imprison a severely disabled person in conditions where she was dangerously cold, risked developing bed sores and was unable to go to the toilet or keep clean without difficulty. (App. No. 33394/96) July 10, 2001

Commentary
It was considered significant that the documentary evidence submitted indicated that the police and prison authorities were not able to cope adequately with the applicant's special needs.

Children

Key Principle: **Corporal punishment of juveniles may amount to a breach of Article 3.**

Tyrer v. U.K. 1978
The applicant, who was convicted of assault by a juvenile court in the Isle of Man, was sentenced to three strokes of the birch when he was 15. He complained to the Commission that the United Kingdom being responsible for the Isle of Man's international relations was in breach of Article 3.

Held: (ECtHR) The facts of the case did not amount to torture or inhuman punishment. It was, however, degrading treatment, and "although the applicant did not suffer any severe or long-lasting physical effects, his punishment—whereby he was treated as an object in the power of the authorities—constituted an assault on precisely that which is one of the main purposes of Article 3 to protect, namely a person's dignity and physical integrity. Neither can it be excluded that the punishment may have had adverse psychological effects. (1978) 2 E.H.R.R. 1

Commentary
Judicial corporal punishment on the mainland had been abolished in 1948 and in Northern Ireland in 1968. Corporal punishment in schools came under challenge in *Campbell and Cosans v. U.K.* (1982) 4 E.H.R.R. 293, an application brought by the mothers of two Scottish school boys threatened by the tawse. Here the court found it had not been established that the pupils had been humiliated or degraded in the eyes of others. However the failure to respect the parents' wishes that their sons should not be beaten was a violation of Protocol 1, Article 2 (see p. 177). A series of cases led to the Government banning corporal punishment in state schools (see *Warwick v. U.K.* (1986) 60 D.R. 5). See *Costello-Roberts v. U.K.* (1995) for the use of corporal punishment in independent schools. In that case the court found no breach of Articles 2 or 8. This case was distinguished from *Tyrer* in that the punishment was given in private, and consisted of three strokes with a rubber-soled slipper on the buttocks through shorts. There the minimal level of severity required by Article 3 had not been reached. See also pp. 7–8, 31, 48, 50, 120.

Key Principle: **States have a positive responsibility to safe-guard children from physical punishment.**

A v. U.K. 1999
The applicant was a boy whose stepfather regularly beat him with a garden cane causing considerable bruising. The father was acquitted of assault on the basis that the beatings amounted to reasonable chastisement. The boy complained that the State had failed to safeguard his rights under Article 3.

Held: (ECtHR) The boy's treatment did reach the level of severity prohibited by the Article and the law allowing "reasonable chastisement" did not provide adequate protection to children's Convention rights. (1999) 27 E.H.R.R. 611

Commentary
At the trial the stepfather had successfully raised the defence of lawful punishment. The prosecution had the burden of proving beyond reasonable doubt that the assault was not lawful. The Government has accepted that the defence of lawful chastisement is too wide.

Z v. U.K. 2001
Four children were neglected and beaten by their parents, despite monitoring by the social services. Proceedings brought by the Official Solicitor on behalf of the children were struck out in the House of Lords on the grounds of public policy. The House of Lords held that local authorities should not be liable in negligence for having failed to safeguard the welfare of children in their area. [2002] 34 E.H.R.R. 3

Held: (ECtHR) The system had failed to protect the applicant from serious, long-term neglect and abuse. This was a violation of Article 3. The courts had failed to provide them with an adequate remedy.

Commentary
These cases make it clear that there is a positive obligation under Article 2 to prevent, investigate and punish private domestic violence. This case was the sequel to the House of Lords decision in *X (Minors) v. Bedfordshire CC* [1995] 2 A.C. 633. (See also pp. 98–9).

Prohibition of Slavery and Forced Labour

Key Principle: **Article 4 of the ECHR—Prohibition of Slavery and forced labour:**

"1 No one shall be held in slavery or servitude.

2 No one shall be required to perform forced or compulsory labour.

3 For the purpose of this article the term 'forced or compulsory labour' shall not include:

  a any work required to be done in the ordinary course of detention imposed according to the provisions of Article 5 of this Convention or during conditional release from such detention;
  b any service of a military character or, in the case of conscientious objectors in countries where they are recognised, service exacted instead of compulsory military service;
  c any service exacted in case of an emergency or calamity threatening the life or well-being of the community;
  d any work or service which forms part of normal civic obligations."

Key Principle: **Military service, even for those who enlist below the age of majority does not generally amount to "slavery or servitude".**

W, X, Y and Z v. U.K.
The applicants had joined the army or navy at the age of 15 or 16 with the consent of their parents. Their contracts were for nine years, which was calculated from the date at which they reached the age of 18 and they could not leave the services before this time other than in "exceptional circumstances". The applicants alleged violations of Articles 6, 8, and 13 as well as 4, the latter on the grounds of relief from "oppressive compulsory service tantamount to the status of servitude".

Held: (Commission) The clause excluding military service expressly from the scope of the terms "forced or compulsory labour" does not forcibly exclude such service in all circumstances from an examination in the light of the prohibition directed at "slavery or servitude". Generally the duty of a soldier whether enlisting before or after the age of majority doesn't amount to an impairment of rights which could come under the terms "slavery or servitude". (1968) 11 Y.B. 562 (App. No. 3435–38/67)

Commentary
In an interesting example of its jurisprudential approach the Commission drew on the history of the provision including Convention Number 29 of the International Labour Organisation on Forced or Compulsory Labour.

Key Principle: **For labour to be forced or compulsory it must be performed involuntarily and the requirement to do the work must be unjust or oppressive or the work itself involve avoidable hardship.**

Van der Mussele v. Belgium 1983
Belgian law required pupil advocates to represent clients without payment. The applicant had provided some 750 hours of unpaid work as a pupil barrister. He alleged violation of Articles 4, 6, 14 and Article 1 of the first Protocol.

Held: (ECtHR) The barrister had entered the profession of his own free will, knowing that *pro bono* work was expected of him. The labour imposed on him was not a "burden which was so excessive or disproportionate to the advantages attached to the future exercise of the profession that the service could not be treated as having been voluntarily accepted". There were no violations. (1984) 6 E.H.R.R. 163

Commentary
The work performed could be considered as a "normal civil obligation". The majority of claims under Article 4 have been brought by serving prisoners.

4. DUE PROCESS AND A FAIR TRIAL IN CRIMINAL COURTS

Detention

Key Principle: **Article 5 of the ECHR—Right to liberty and security:**

"1 Everyone has the right to liberty and security of person. No one shall be deprived of his liberty save in the following cases and in accordance with a procedure prescribed by law:

a the lawful detention of a person after conviction by a competent court;

b the lawful arrest or detention of a person for non-compliance with the lawful order of a court or in order to secure the fulfilment of any obligation prescribed by law;

c the lawful arrest or detention of a person effected for the purpose of bringing him before the competent legal authority on reasonable suspicion of having committed an offence or when it is reasonably considered necessary to prevent his committing an offence or fleeing after having done so;

d the detention of a minor by lawful order for the purpose of educational supervision or his lawful detention for the purpose of bringing him before the competent legal authority;

e the lawful detention of persons for the prevention of the spreading of infectious diseases, of persons of unsound mind, alcoholics or drug addicts or vagrants;

f the lawful arrest or detention of a person to prevent his effecting an unauthorised entry into the country or of a person against whom action is being taken with a view to deportation or extradition.

2 Everyone who is arrested shall be informed promptly, in a language which he understands, of the reasons for his arrest and of any charge against him.

3 Everyone arrested or detained in accordance with the provisions of paragraph 1.c of this article shall be brought promptly before a judge or other officer authorised by law to exercise judicial power and shall be entitled to trial within a reasonable time or to release pending trial. Release may be conditioned by guarantees to appear for trial.

4 Everyone who is deprived of his liberty by arrest or detention shall be entitled to take proceedings by which the lawfulness of his detention shall be decided speedily by a court and his release ordered if the detention is not lawful.

5 Everyone who has been the victim of arrest or detention in contravention of the provisions of this article shall have an enforceable right to compensation."

Key Principle: **No one shall be deprived of his liberty save under the exceptions listed in Article 5 and in accordance with a procedure prescribed by law.**

de Wilde v. Belgium

The applicants were arrested as vagrants and held without trial for up to 21 months. All had unsuccessfully petitioned for release but had not appealed since Belgian case-law appeared to rule out an appeal from a magistrate's administrative decision. They complained of a violation of their rights under Article 5(4), on the basis that there was no judicial remedy for their imprisonment.

Held: Article 5(4) had been breached because the applicants had no remedy before a court against the detention orders. The Convention required that where a person was deprived of his liberty by an administrative decision he was entitled to have the lawfulness of his detention supervised by a court. (1979–1980) 1 E.H.R.R. 373 ECHR

Commentary

The cases illustrates that even if an individual waives his rights under the Article and agrees to his detention that detention can still be unlawful. The court stated "the right to liberty is too important in a 'democratic society' within the meaning of the Convention for a person to lose the benefit of the protection of the Convention for the single reason that he gives himself up to be taken into detention."

Key Principle: **An authority should furnish acceptable evidence of the grounds for "reasonable suspicion" of an individual having committed an offence for which he is being detained.**

Fox, Campbell and Hartley v. U.K.

The applicants were detained in Northern Ireland for periods between 30 and 44 hours under a power to arrest without warrant "any person suspected of being a terrorist". They were informed in general terms of the reason for their arrest when they were held, and learned the details during interrogation.

Held: The legislation allowed for arrest on "reasonable" (which in domestic law meant "honestly held") suspicion. Reasonableness depended on the circumstances. Past terrorist convictions were not in themselves enough to justify arrest. The applicants' rights under Article 5(1) had been violated. (1990) 13 E.H.R.R. 157

Commentary

The court accepted that "reasonable suspicion" was not necessarily "a genuine and bona fide suspicion". In terrorist crimes in particular the police may have to act on the basis of information which cannot be revealed to the suspect. In *Brogan v. U.K.* (1989) also the court was prepared to accept that reasonable suspicion of being a terrorist satisfied the requirements of the article. Although the power was expressed in subjective terms the question is whether, as a matter of fact, the suspicion was based on reasonable grounds.

Key Principle: **Anyone arrested should be brought promptly before a judge or other judicial officer and should be tried within a reasonable time or released pending trial.**

Brogan v. U.K. (1989)

Four applicants were detained under section 12 of the Prevention of Terrorism Act 1978 and held for periods of between four and 16 days without being charged or brought before a magistrate.

Held: The Convention required that suspects be produced "promptly". The court accepted that subject to the existence of adequate safeguards, the context of terrorism in Northern Ireland had the effect of prolonging the allowable detention period. But four days and six hours was too long. (1989) 11 E.H.R.R. 117

Commentary
As a result of this case the United Kingdom issued a notice of derogation (see p. 8).

Key Principle: **A detained person has a right to have the lawfulness of his detention reviewed by a body independent of the executive and the parties.**

T v. U.K.; V v. U.K.
The applicants had been convicted of the abduction and murder of a two-year-old boy. They had been 10 at the time of the murder and 11 at the time of the Crown Court trial. They were sentenced to be detained indefinitely during her Majesty's pleasure and according to English law had first to serve a tariff period to satisfy the requirements of retribution and deterrence. Detainees would be released on expiry of the tariff unless, in the view of the parole board, they were a danger to the public. The Home Secretary's tariff of 15 years for each of the applicants had been quashed by the House of Lords and no new tariff had been set. The applicants claimed first that their trial and sentence was a violation of Article 3 of the ECHR; secondly that they had been denied a fair trial under Article 6, and the fact that it was a government minister who was responsible for setting the tariff was a violation of Article 6; thirdly that the sentence imposed was a breach of Article 5 and that there was a further breach of that article in that they had been denied the opportunity to have the lawfulness of their detention examined by a judicial body.

Held: (ECtHR) There was no breach of Article 3 since the age of 10 could not be said to be so young as to differ disproportionately to the age limit set for trial by other European states. There had been a breach of the right to a fair trial and that the setting of the tariff and the absence of judicial scrutiny of it were also violations of Articles 6 and 5. (1999) 30 E.H.R.R. 121

Commentary
In March 2000 the Home Secretary stated that legislation would be introduced in line with this decision and that for existing cases he proposed a fresh review of tariffs in line with the principles of the judgment. He would adopt the recommendations of the Lord Chief Justice; such a new tariff career was set in the cases of T and V and the parole board was to make a decision about their release. Successful challenges under Article 5(4) have also been made in relation to continuing detention in discretionary period life sentences (see *Weeks v. U.K.* (1988) 10 E.H.R.R. 293, *Thynne v. U.K.* (1990) 3 E.H.R.R. 666. The court has stressed that it is crucial to recognise that circumstances could change over time. As a result of *Thynne* the United Kingdom introduced oral hearings to consider discretionary life paroles. These have the power to direct a prisoner's release when he is no longer dangerous. (See also *Wynne v. U.K.* and *R. v. Secretary of State for the Home Department, ex parte Anderson, The Times*, November 16, 2001. In *Anderson* the Court of Appeal held that the Home Secretary was entitled to fix the tariff for life imprisonment since the requirements of Article 6 were satisfied by the court which imposed the sentence. The system was subject to judicial review and the court could not act contrary to the Convention. The Strasbourg Court will review this issue in *Stafford v. U.K.*).

Bail

Key Principle: **Facts relevant to a decision on whether a defendant had broken a condition of bail did not have to be proved to the criminal standard to comply with Article 5.**

R. v. Havering Magistrates' Court, *ex parte* DPP
There were two joined cases concerning the effect of the HRA on the Bail Act 1976. The defendants in the two cases were arrested for breach of bail conditions and brought before the magistrates. In the first case the justices held that Articles 5 and 6 ECHR applied and that the prosecution was obliged to call oral evidence to prove the breach of bail conditions. In the second case the justices held that Article 5 but not Article 6 applied and oral evidence was not required. The applications

were for judicial review by the prosecution in the first case and by the defendant in the second as to whether the ECHR required formal proof to be given of a breach of bail conditions.

Held: (DC) The rights under Article 6 had no relevance to proceedings under section 7 of the 1976 Act. While Article 5 was relevant to proceedings under section 7, Articles 5 and 6 related to two separate sets of proceedings which had different objects and the procedural requirements of Article 6 were not to be assimilated to the considerations relevant to Article 5. Article 5 did not require the underlying facts relevant to detention under section 7 to be proved to the criminal standard of proof or that only evidence which would be admissible at trial could be relied on. To comply with Article 5 it was necessary for the magistrates to evaluate the material and its nature in the light of the serious potential consequences to the defendant and form an honest and rational opinion. [2001] 1 W.L.R. 805

Commentary
The court here applied the existing law in *R. v. Liverpool City Justices, ex parte DPP* [1993] Q.B. 233. In *Caballero v. U.K., The Times* February 29, 2000, the then existing bail conditions were found to be a violation of Article 5(3) and as a result section 25 of the Criminal Justice and Public Order Act was amended. In one of the earliest cases under the HRA, *Burgess v. Home Office* [2001] 1 W.L.R. 93 the Court of Appeal found that Article 5 "added nothing to the claimant's case". It was held that the detention of the claimant, who was required to surrender to custody from one hour before each day's hearing until half an hour after the court rose for five days during his criminal trial did not entitle him to have that period taken into account on sentence.

Key Principle: **A new offence charged on the same facts could give rise to fresh custody time limit and was not incompatible with Articles 5(1) or 5(3).**

R. v. Leeds Crown Court, ex parte Wardle
In July 1998 a man died during a burglary or robbery at his home. The defendants were originally charged with murder and a new charge of manslaughter was substituted on the last day of the custody time limit for the murder charge. The magistrates'

court found that a new custody time limit had thereby been created. The decision was upheld by the judge, although he held that if the old custody time limits had applied it would not have been appropriate to have extended them, as the prosecution had not acted with due expedition. The applicants sought judicial review of the decision submitting that it was an abuse of process that new custody time limits should be created in these circumstances. The Divisional Court had found that it was not an abuse of process for the prosecution to change the charge on the last day of the custody time limit thereby creating a new custody limit, even when the old custody time limit would not have been extended because the prosecution had not acted with expedition. The applicants also applied for writs of habeas corpus.

Held: (HL) When a new charge had been laid in the magistrates' court on the last day of the custody time limit of the original charge, the true question was whether the new charge had been brought solely for the purpose of avoiding a custody time limit and the prosecutor was required to demonstrate why the bringing of the new charge was necessary. Murder and manslaughter were distinct in law and were separate offences attracting separate custody time limits. It was plain that Parliament had intended there to be limits on the period during which a person could be detained. It was recognised that where there was an abuse of process by adding additional or substituted charges, a new period of custody time limits did not operate. A mere change in the details of the charge did not of itself mean that time would begin to run again. However, where the new charge was plainly distinct from any original charges, the new charge attracted its own separate time limit. It would clearly be an abuse of process to bring a new charge simply to keep an accused in custody for a longer period. However, if the purpose was genuinely to introduce a new charge on a revised assessment of the case, the fact that the accused began a new custody period did not in itself constitute an abuse of process. There was no breach of Article 5 ECHR as D had been deprived of his liberty in accordance with a procedure prescribed by law and the domestic law complied with the general requirements of the Convention. Appeal dismissed. [2001] 2 W.L.R. 865

Commentary
This is a controversial decision and some commentators expect a challenge in Strasbourg.

Presence of Defendants

Key Principle: **Fair procedure will generally, but not always, require the presence in person of the party concerned.**

Monnell and Morris v. U.K.
The applicants had persisted in hopeless appeals against conviction and sentence and the Appeal Court ordered in their absence that part of the time they had already served since conviction should not count towards their sentences. They claimed this was a violation of Article 5(1).

Held: (ECtHR) Under English law a sentence of imprisonment was to be served subject to any order for loss of time the Court of Appeal might make. The power to order loss of time served a legitimate purpose of discouraging futile appeals. Article 5(1) had not been violated. The applicants had been warned that they might lose time if they persisted with their appeals and had not been denied the benefit of fair procedure. (1988) 10 E.H.R.R. 205

Commentary
In this case the principle of "equality of arms" was protected since neither the applicants nor the prosecution were represented by a barrister or by a solicitor before the court.

Right to a Fair Trial

Key Principle: **Article 6 of the ECHR—Right to a fair trial:**

"1 In the determination of his civil rights and obligations or of any criminal charge against him, everyone is entitled to a fair and public hearing within a reasonable time by an independent and impartial tribunal established by law. Judgment shall be pronounced publicly but the press and public may be excluded from all or part of the trial in the interests of morals, public order or national security in a democratic society, where the interests of juveniles or the protection of the private life of the parties so require, or to the extent strictly necessary in the opinion of the court in special circumstances where publicity would prejudice the interests of justice.

2 Everyone charged with a criminal offence shall be presumed innocent until proved guilty according to law.

3 Everyone charged with a criminal offence has the following minimum rights:

    a to be informed promptly, in a language which he understands and in detail, of the nature and cause of the accusation against him;

    b to have adequate time and facilities for the preparation of his defence;

    c to defend himself in person or through legal assistance of his own choosing or, if he has not sufficient means to pay for legal assistance, to be given it free when the interests of justice so require;

    d to examine or have examined witnesses against him and to obtain the attendance and examination of witnesses on his behalf under the same conditions as witnesses against him;

    e to have the free assistance of an interpreter if he cannot understand or speak the language used in court."

Key Principle: **The accused's right to a fair trial is not to be subordinated to the public interest in the detection and suppression of crime.**

Montgomery v. HM Advocate; Coulter v. HM Advocate
Three white men, the defendants and C, were charged with murdering an Asian youth. Only C was indicted and at trial he raised a special defence of incrimination, naming the defendants as the perpetrators. C was convicted of assaulting, but acquitted of murdering, the victim. After the verdict the trial judge criticised the prosecution for not having had all three tried together. The judge's remarks were publicly criticised by the Lord Advocate, the head of the Scottish prosecution system. After a public campaign the defendants were indicted for the Asian's murder. They complained that the pre-trial publicity had made it impossible for them to have a fair trial as required

by Article 6 ECHR. Further publicity about the case was banned some seven weeks after the defendants were indicted. The trial judge rejected the contention that the defendants would not be able to have a fair trial. The defendants appealed.

Held: (PC) Dismissing the appeal, that the only issue to be considered under Article 6 was the defendants' right to a fair trial, and considerations of the public interest did not arise. The decisive question was whether the doubts raised about the tribunal's impartiality were objectively justified. It had to be borne in mind that the trial judge could warn the jury to ignore prejudicial pre-trial publicity, and that listening to witnesses and thinking about the evidence would be likely to have a greater impact on the jury than their recollections of matters they had read in the past. [2001] 2 W.L.R. 779

The content of a criminal charge

Key Principle: **A criminal charge is an official notification to an individual by the competent authority of an allegation that he has committed a criminal offence and covers measures which substantially affect the situation of a suspect.**

Campbell and Fell v. United Kingdom
The applicants, in prison for terrorist offences, faced disciplinary proceedings as a result of disturbances, were convicted and lost privileges and remission. They alleged that the proceedings were the determination of a "criminal charge" and so should have complied with Article 6.

Held: (ECtHR) The classification by the national state of the nature of proceedings was not decisive although there was a necessary distinction between disciplinary and criminal matters. The court was entitled to consider the nature of the proceedings and, taking account of the gravity of the offences charged, and the severity of the penalty the applicants risked, Article 6 was applicable. (1985) 7 E.H.R.R. 165

Commentary
The question of what is or is not a criminal charge is not defined in the ECHR and therefore must be derived from the jurisprudence.

The court was faced here with deciding whether the disciplinary adjudications of the prison governor attracted the protection of Article 6. In other cases the Strasbourg court had afforded Article 6 protection to searches of premises but not to the questioning of witnesses. The determination of the proceedings is crucial since the complete protection of Article 6 is only afforded to criminal hearings not civil, see *Benham v. U.K.* (pp. 82, 193).

In *Eckle v. Germany* (1983) 5 E.H.R.R. 1 being charged was defined as "the official notification given to an individual by the competent authority of an allegation that he has committed a criminal offence". It was made clear in *Neumeister v. Austria (No. 1)* (1979–1980) 1 E.H.R.R. 91 that the period covers the whole of the time for the proceedings to be completed, including appeal proceedings.

Key Principle: **An award of additional days' imprisonment as a result of prison disciplinary hearings did not mean that the proceedings should be regarded as "criminal" for the purposes of Article 6.**

R. (Carroll) v. Secretary of State for Home Department
The appeals arose from dismissals of applications for judicial review by serving prisoners. They argued that internal prison disciplinary hearings which resulted in further days in prison should be subject to Article 6. It was also argued that the requirement of legality meant that prison officers should give reasons for squat searches which otherwise violated Article 8.

Held: (CA) The proceedings were disciplinary under domestic law; the additional days imprisonment did not add to the sentence they merely postponed release on licence and the punishment powers were not disproportionate. Article 6 did not apply. Individual prison officers should decide if it was necessary to give reasons for the searches. *The Times*, August 16, 2001

Commentary
This is a narrowly based decision which does not appear to follow the reasoning of *Campbell and Fell*. It has been criticised as leaving the interpretation of the provisions of the Convention to prison officers rather than the courts (see Commentary in the journal *Human Rights* (December 2001) p. 243).

Key Principle: **The imposition of a civil evasion penalty in respect of value added tax or excise duty gave rise to a "criminal charge" within Article 6(1) of the European Convention on Human Rights.**

Han & Yau and Others v. Customs & Excise Commissioners

This was a trial of a preliminary issue in relation to three appeals concerning whether the imposition of a civil evasion penalty on the three appellants under section 60 of the Value Added Tax Act 1994 (VATA) or section 8 of the Finance Act 1994 (FA) gave rise to a "criminal charge" within Article 6(1) of the European Convention on Human Rights. In each case no point was taken that the penalty in question was imposed before the HRA 1998 came into force. In each appeal the appellant taxpayer was appealing from a civil penalty assessment which had been imposed upon him for alleged dishonest evasion of tax. Each appellant contended by way of preliminary issue that the imposition of such a penalty gave rise to "criminal charges" within the meaning of Article 6 of the Convention. The tribunal had determined the issue in favour of the taxpayers by reference to the three criteria laid down in *Engel & Ors v. The Netherlands* (1976) 1 E.H.R.R. 706, namely: (i) the classification of the proceedings in United Kingdom law; (ii) the nature of the offence; and (iii) the severity of the penalty that might be imposed.

Held: (CA) The court accepted that the imposition of a civil penalty gave rise to a criminal charge within the meaning of Article 6 of the Convention. In particular, the court accepted that (a) the civil penalty regime replaced the earlier criminal regime; (b) the offence to which the penalty related involved fraud/ dishonesty; and (c) the amount of the penalty that could be imposed was substantial and its purpose was punitive and deterrent. [2001] 1 W.L.R. 2253

Commentary

The labelling of the charge here as civil as also in cases under the regime of the Inland Revenue suits the administrative convenience of government departments and has some advantages to defendants in that for example they do not give rise to a criminal record. The court referred to Strasbourg cases in its judgment including *AP, MP and TP v. Switzerland* (1998) 26 E.H.R.R. 541 and *Georgiou v. U.K.* [2001] S.T.C. 80 as being at the heart of the case law. It did not consider it was now appropriate to place the jurisprudence of the United Kingdom out on a limb in an area where the Strasbourg cases had sought to develop an autonomous integrated test. The previous case law indicated that there are three criteria to be taken into account when it is being decided whether a person was "charged with a criminal offence" for the purposes of Article 6. They were the classification of the offence under national law, the nature of the offence, and the nature and degree of severity of the penalty the person concerned risked. These requirements were not a formula for a three stage test. They were factors which should be taken into account in examining whether on the facts as a whole the measure should be treated as criminal. See also *King v. Walden (Inspector of Taxes), The Times* June 12, 2001.

Key Principle: **Confiscation proceedings arising from drug trafficking offences do not concern a criminal charge.**

McIntosh v. HM Advocate
The defendant had been convicted of being concerned in the supply of heroin. The prosecutor applied for a confiscation order against him under the Proceeds of Crime (Scotland) Act 1995. This allowed the court to make assumptions about of the source of property of the convicted drug dealer. The Scottish High Court of Justiciary held that the presumption of innocence was violated. HM Advocate appealed.

Held: (PC) The confiscation order was not a criminal charge. Even if the respondent appellant had been entitled to take advantage of Article 6(2) his right to a fair trial would not have been violated in this case. [2001] 3 W.L.R. 107

Commentary
The Privy Council referred to the reasoning in *R. v. Benjafield* [2001] 2 Cr.App.R. 87 where it was held that confiscation orders were criminal charges but that Article 6 was not violated by the imposition of a reverse burden of proof since the legislation was a proportionate response to a grave social evil. Perhaps surprisingly in *McIntosh* it also stated that in concluding that Article 6(2) had

no application to the prosecutor's application for a confiscation order the result did not leave the respondent unprotected since "he was entitled to all the protection afforded him by Article 6(1) which applied at all stages, the common law of Scotland and the language of the statute" (*per* Lord Bingham).

Key Principle: **Confiscation orders do not amount to criminal charges but the defendant is entitled to a fair proceeding under Article 6(1).**

Phillips v. U.K.
The applicant who had been convicted of importation of cannabis was subject to a drug confiscation order under the Drug Trafficking Act 1994. This empowers a court to assume that all property held by a person convicted of a drug trafficking offence in the previous three years represented the proceeds of drug trafficking. He complained that the application of the statutory presumption violated his right to the presumption of innocence under Article 6(2).

Held: (ECtHR) (1) A person against whom a confiscation order was made was not a person charged with a criminal offence. (2) A person's right in a criminal case to be presumed innocent forms part of the general notion of a fair hearing under Article 6(1). (2001) Crim.L.R. 817

Commentary
The court endorsed the approach of the Privy Council in *HM Advocate v. McIntosh*. The judgment raises quite difficult problems of interpretation. Although confiscation proceedings do not concern a criminal charge it appears the ECtHR still applies the procedural safeguards of Article 6(1) since "In addition to being specifically mentioned in Article 6(2) a person's right in a criminal case to be presumed innocent and to require the prosecution to bear the onus of proving the allegations against him or her forms part of the general notion of a fair hearing under Article 6(1)". The court considered that an issue relating to fair procedure might arise in drug confiscation orders but on the facts of this case the operation of the statutory assumption did not violate the notion of a fair hearing under Article 6(1).

Reasonable Time

Key Principle: **In the determination of any criminal charge against him everyone is entitled to a fair and public hearing within a reasonable time.**

Attorney-General's Reference (No. 2 of 2001)

A judge had stayed an indictment against seven defendants facing charges of violent disorder on the grounds that to proceed would be a breach of Article 6(1) due to delay between the interview and the summons. The Attorney-General asked two questions of law: (1) whether criminal proceedings could be stayed on the grounds that there had been a violation of the reasonable time requirement in Article 6(1) in circumstances where the accused could not demonstrate any prejudice from the delay; and (2) when in the determination of whether a criminal charge had been heard within a reasonable time the relevant period began.

Held: (CA) Time does not run from an interview in terms of Article 6(1). Staying proceedings should only be granted in situations where to continue with the trial would be an abuse of the process of the court. Other remedies were available such as a reduction in sentence or compensation. Absent prejudice, there would normally be no justification for a stay. [2001] 1 W.L.R. 1809

Commentary

Most cases on delay in the Strasbourg Court involve Italy. In *Howarth v. U.K.* (2001) 31 E.H.R.R. 37 the court held that a delay of two years between the the original sentence and the imposition of a greater sentence following an Attorney-General's reference was excessive. It is interesting to note that the Crown Court does not have power to award compensation for breach of the Convention. See also *McLean v. HM Advocate* [2000] U.K.H.R.R. 73 where it was held that delay without prejudice can result in proceedings being staged.

Access to the criminal courts

Key Principle: **There is no power to extend the time allowed for the prosecution to apply for leave to appeal from the Court of Appeal to the House of Lords.**

R. v. Weir

The Court of Appeal had quashed the defendant's conviction for murder, burglary and assault on the grounds that the DNA evidence used to convict him had been inadmissible under section 64 (3 b) of the Police and Criminal Evidence Act 1984 (PACE) as amended by section 57 of the Criminal Justice and Public Order Act 1994. The Court of Appeal certified the point of law of general public importance but the DPP lodged his application for leave to appeal to the House of Lords one day after expiry of the 14-day time limit laid down in section 34 of the Criminal Appeal Act 1968 and the application was rejected by the Judicial Office. Subsequently in another case (Attorney-General's Reference No. 3 of 1999 [2001] 2 W.L.R. 56) the House ruled that pursuant to section 78 of PACE trial judges had a discretionary power to admit evidence of the type used to convict the defendant. The DPP lodged a petition seeking leave to apply to the House for leave to appeal on the grounds that the House had a discretion to extend the statutory time limit and that it would be contrary to the HRA for the time limit not to be extended.

Held: (HL) The appellate jurisdiction of the House in criminal matters was statutory and by section 34 of the 1968 Act Parliament had provided for time to be extended on application for leave to appeal by a defendant but not by that of the prosecutor. The situation did not engage the human rights of the DPP in any way. [2001] 1 W.L.R. 421

Commentary

In this case the House of Lords considered Articles 2, 3 and 8 as well as 6 and held that if the Court of Appeal made an erroneous decision in law in favour of a defendant it could be corrected by the House of Lords. The House of Lords underlined here the main purpose of the Convention as being to protect the individual against oppressive state action. It stated: "the Convention was concerned to protect the rights of private citizens against abuse of power by the state and could not be interpreted as strengthening the rights of prosecutors against private individuals".

Impartiality

Key Principle: **The accused is entitled to an independent and impartial tribunal established by law.**

Sander v. U.K.
After a trial where the Asian applicant was the defendant a juror had transmitted a note to the judge indicating that another juror had made racist comments during deliberations. The judge had given the jury a redirection. The applicant was convicted. He alleged a violation of Article 6.

Held: (ECtHR) The judge's decision to deal with the allegation of racial bias in the jury by means of a redirection rather than a discharge did constitute an infringement of the right to a fair trial as guaranteed by Article 6(1). *The Times,* May 12, 2000

Commentary
The court considered that the judge should have reacted in a more robust manner than merely seeking vague assurances that the jurors could set aside their prejudices and try the case solely on the evidence. The judge had not therefore provided sufficient guarantees to exclude any objectively justified or legitimate doubts as to the impartiality of the court. In *Mills v. U.K.* (App. No. 35686/97) June 5, 2001 the court found there had been a violation of Article 6(1). The applicant who served in the army was tried by a court martial. The court held that this did not meet the requirement of independence and impartiality under Article 6(1) in view particularly of the central part played by the commanding officer.

Key Principle: **Magistrates should not exercise powers to bind over defendants to be of good behaviour in respect of their conduct in court.**

Practice Direction (Magistrates' Courts: Contempt)
Guidance was sought as to the way to deal with contempt in the
face of the court where the same bench was deciding the
contempt and the substantive trial.

Held: (DC) Detailed guidance was set out. In particular where
contempt was not admitted the justices' power was limited to
making arrangement for a trial to take place. They should not at
this stage make findings against the defendant. The trial should
take place at the earliest opportunity and should be before a
bench of justices other than those justices before whom the
alleged contempt took place. The accused's rights under Article
6 should be respected. [2001] 1 W.L.R. 1254

Commentary
The Direction gave very specific advice for situations where the
courts had previously adopted a different position but where now
the Convention rights must be observed.

Key Principle: **It was not necessarily a breach of Article 6 for
the same bench to decide the public interest immunity (PII)
hearing and the substantive trial.**

R (Acton Youth Court) v. DPP
The District Judge at Acton youth court had heard an *ex parte*
application for a PII certificate and had ruled in favour of the
prosecution that the evidence should not be disclosed to the
defence. He had disqualified himself from hearing the trial. The
DPP applied for judicial review.

Held: (DC) Review allowed. The general rule was that justices
who had ruled on PII should use their discretion as to whether
or not to remit the trial to another bench on the basis of whether
or not any reasonable and fair-minded person could reasonably
have suspected the defendant could not have a fair trial before
the same bench. The procedure in the Crown Court could be
followed and the case should not be remitted as a matter of
practice. *The Times*, June 21, 2001

Commentary
The court referred to *R. v. Stipendiary Magistrates for Norfolk, ex
parte Taylor* (1997) 161 J.P. 773 as setting out the proceedings for

the Crown Court. It noted that the European Court had endorsed this approach in *Fitt v. U.K.* (2000) 30 E.H.R.R. 480 and there was no reason why such an approach should not be followed in the magistrates' courts.

Right to Silence

Key Principle: **The right to remain silent under police questioning and the privilege against self-incrimination are generally recognised international standards which lie at the heart of the notion of a fair procedure under Article 6.**

Funke v. France
Customs officers searched the applicant's home to obtain details of his overseas assets and seized documents. The operation did not result in criminal proceedings under the relevant financial dealing regulations, but there were parallel proceedings for disclosure of documents and interim orders. The applicant was convicted and fined for failing to provide statements of his overseas bank accounts.

Held: The applicant's conviction was an attempt to compel him to provide evidence of other offences he had allegedly committed. His right to remain silent and not to incriminate himself had been infringed. (1993) 16 E.H.R.R. 297 ECHR

Key Principle: **Where answers are given on the course of compulsory proceedings the use of them by the prosecution at a subsequent criminal trial may violate Article 6.**

Saunders v. U.K.
A company chief executive was questioned by Department of Trade inspectors investigating a takeover battle. He was obliged by law to answer their questions on pain of up to two years' imprisonment. The inspectors recommended prosecution and transcripts of his interrogation by the inspectors were used against him at trial.

Held: (ECtHR) The use of the transcripts at trial violated the applicant's right not to be forced to incriminate himself. The right was primarily concerned with respecting the will of the accused to remain silent. (1997) 23 E.H.R.R. 313

Commentary

The court saw no inherent objection to legislation which compels parties to answer questions in the course of non-judicial inquiries but "the public interest cannot be invoked to justify the use of answers compulsorily obtained in a non-judicial investigation to incriminate the accused during trial proceedings." It did not extend to evidence which might be obtained by compulsion but was independent of the suspect's will, such as breath samples. In the wake of this decision the Attorney-General issued guidelines designed to prevent the Crown from using what were known as items of "derivative evidence" obtained in extra-judicial investigations. The Youth Justice and Criminal Evidence Act 1999 Sched. 3 has amended those provisions such as section 434 of the Companies Act 1985 which formerly purported to render admissible in subsequent criminal proceedings evidence procured by compulsion during investigations. Subsequently the applications of the three co-defendants of Saunders succeeded on identical grounds at Strasbourg, see *ILJ, GMR and AKP v. U.K.*, *The Times* October 13, 2000. In *R. v. Lyons* (see p. 26) the Court of Appeal held that the HRA did not have retrospective effect so as to affect the convictions of the men involved in the Guinness scandal, Lyons, Parnes, Ronson and Saunders. In *R. v. Hertfordshire County Council, ex parte Green Environmental Industries Ltd* [2000] A.C. 412 Lord Hoffman acknowledged that although the relevant statute, namely the Environmental Protection Act 1990, did not expressly provide that answers obtained in non-judicial inquiries would be admissible in any subsequent prosecution, the trial judge if faced with such a request from the prosecution will be required under the HRA to consider whether such derivative evidence conforms with Article 6. If it does not it should be excluded under section 78 of the PACE.

Key Principle: **The right to remain silent is not an absolute.**

Murray v. U.K.

The applicant had been found guilty of aiding and abetting unlawful imprisonment after being arrested in an IRA safe house. He was interviewed without a solicitor and remained silent. The trial judge informed the applicant that because of his failure to account for his presence at the house and because he had not given evidence at trial, he had drawn adverse inferences under the Criminal Evidence (Northern Ireland) Order 1988. The applicant claimed violations of Article 6.

Held: (ECtHR) The right to remain silent under police questioning and the privilege against self incrimination are generally recognised international standards which lie at the heart of the notion of fair procedure under Article 6. But these immunities were not absolutes. There was no breach of Article 6 in the drawing of inferences from silence but there was a breach in that the suspect's access to a solicitor had been delayed. (1996) 22 E.H.R.R. 29

Commentary

The provisions in the Order were applied to the mainland in sections 34 to 38 of the Criminal Justice and Public Order Act (CJPOA) 1994. While refusing to uphold the right to remain silent in the face of police questioning as an absolute the decision makes it clear that the drawing of adverse inferences when the suspect had not had access to legal advice prior to the failure to reply to questions will breach Article 6. The court made it clear that its findings were confined to the particular facts of the case in particular that the trier of fact was a judge in a Diplock Court who had expertise to appraise the evidence. The court stated that it would be incompatible with Articles 6(1) and (2) "to base a conviction solely or mainly on the accused's silence or refusal to answer questions".

Key Principle: **The fact that an accused has been advised to remain silent by his solicitor is one of the relevant factors to be weighed in the balance when assessing the fairness of the trial but does not in itself render the trial unfair.**

Condron v. U.K.

A solicitor refused to allow his clients to be interviewed about a suspected offence of supplying heroin because he believed that they were suffering from withdrawal symptoms and therefore unfit to be interviewed. The doctors called to examine them thought otherwise. At the trial the two accused relied on facts they could have told the police at interview. The trial judge had failed to direct the jury along the lines recommended by the Judicial Studies Board to the effect that if they concluded, having regard to any explanation advanced to explain the accused's silence or the absence of explanation, that the accused's silence can only sensibly be attributed to the accused's having no answer to the case against him or no answer likely to stand up to cross examination they may draw an adverse inference against him. The Court of Appeal refused despite this to overturn the conviction because it found that the evidence against the defendant was overwhelming. The applicants alleged violations of Article 6.

Held: (ECtHR) The applicants had not had a fair trial since the Court of Appeal should not have found that the conviction was safe despite the erroneous direction of the judge to the jury. Since the court could not know what part the silence played in allowing the jury to come to its decision it should have allowed the appeal. [2000] 8 B.H.R.C. 290

Commentary

The ruling makes it unclear under what circumstances the drawing of adverse inferences will be a violation of Article 6. The principle from *Murray* clearly underlines the importance of legal advice which the domestic decision in *Condron* undermined but the Strasbourg ruling in *Condron* does not give guidance on when a no comment interview based on legal advice should be excluded or as to the reasons which might be regarded as sound for advising a suspect to remain silent. Even if the accused's solicitor advises him to remain silent, the drawing of adverse inferences is not necessarily a violation. The crucial question is that the judge should give specific directions to the jury on what adverse inferences, if any, might be drawn. The absence of such a direction will constitute a violation of Article 6(1).

Key Principle: **Although the overall fairness of a criminal trial could not be compromised the rights enshrined in Article 6 were not absolute.**

Stott (Procurator Fiscal, Dunfermline) v. Brown

The defendant was arrested at a supermarket on suspicion of stealing a bottle of gin. Police were called and noticed that the defendant appeared to have been drinking. They asked how she had come to the store and she told them she had come by car. She was arrested and taken to a police station where she was required under section 172 of the Road Traffic Act 1988 to say who had been driving the car when she came to the supermarket. She admitted she had been the driver, was breathalysed and charged with driving with excess alcohol. She maintained it was contrary to Article 6(1) of the ECHR for the prosecution to rely at her trial on her admission that she had been driving, since it had been compulsorily obtained. The High Court of Justiciary allowed her appeal against conviction on that ground. On appeal by the prosecutor.

Held: (PC) Allowing the appeal, that the right to a fair trial under Article 6 was absolute and could not be compromised, but the privilege against self-incrimination was not absolute, since it was a right implied from Article 6, and could be limited, provided the limitation was proportionate to achieving its aim. There was a clear public interest in enforcing drink-driving legislation. Section 172 of the Road Traffic Act allowed for the putting of one simple question subject to a moderate and non-custodial penalty for failure to answer, and improper coercion could not be used to obtain an answer. It was not incompatible with the Convention for the defendant's answer to be used against her at trial. [2001] 2 W.L.R. 819

Commentary

In this instance some balancing of rights seemed to be necessary. Lord Bingham stated that the ECHR had recognised the need for a fair balance between the general interest of the community and the personal rights of the individual. It was permissible to qualify the right in Article 6 if any qualification was reasonably directed by the national authorities. Commentators have contrasted the decision here and that in *Montgomery* (see example in Marshall, "Things We Can Say About Rights" (2001) *Public Law* at 207. By contrast to the approach in *Stott*, *Montgomery* seemed to suggest that the right to a fair trial is compromised if any balancing of the public interest is allowed. It is arguable that although the overall unqualified right cannot be balanced any or all of its constituent elements can be balanced as long as the response is proportionate.

Presumption of Innocence

Key Principle: **Everyone charged with a criminal offence shall be presumed innocent until proved guilty according to law but did not preclude the imposition of presumptions of fact and law.**

Saliabiaku v. France 1988
The applicant was convicted of smuggling prohibited goods. The prosecution had proved that he was in possession of the goods, but relied on a presumption in the criminal code that a person in possession of prohibited goods was criminally liable.

Held: (ECtHR) Presumptions of fact or law were not in principle contrary to the Convention, though states were obliged to remain within reasonable limits in making such presumptions. It had been open to the applicant to prove *force majeure* and obtain acquittal or to plead mitigating circumstances. Article 6(2) had not been violated. 13 E.H.R.R. 379

Commentary
The implications of this controversial decision are that the existing common law position (see *Woolmington v. DPP*) meets up with the requirement of Article 6 in accepting that the burden of proof could shift by implication on occasion. In *R. v. DPP, ex parte Kebilene* (1999) the House of Lords was asked to consider whether the reverse burden provisions in the Prevention of Terrorism Act violated Article 6(2). In the Divisional Court Lord Bingham had declared that these sections "in a blatant and obvious way" undermined the presumption of innocence. The House of Lords did not pronounce on this point since it was decided that the matter was not reviewable. However their Lordships took a pragmatic approach to the shifting of the burden of proof. Lord Hope stated: "As a matter of general principle . . . a fair balance must be struck between the demands of the general interest of the community and the protection of the fundamental rights of the individual." A relevant factor to consider was whether the defendant was being required to prove an essential element of the offence or establish a special defence or exception, which would be less objectionable. (See also pp. 6, 26).

Key Principle: It may be contrary to the ECtHR to interpret legislation so as to impose the legal burden of proof on the defendant in criminal trials.

R. v. Lambert, Ali and Jordan
For facts see p. 4.

Held: (HL, *obiter*) It was not justifiable to use section 28 of the Misuse of Drugs Act 1971 so as to transfer the legal burden on the accused and require him to prove he did not know the bag contained a controlled drug. It was possible to construe section 28 as imposing an evidential rather than a legal burden and such a requirement was not a violation of the Convention. On the facts if the trial judge had given the direction to the jury that the burden on the accused was only an evidential burden the jury would have reached the same result. The conviction should not be quashed. [2001] 3 W.L.R. 206

Commentary
This was a majority decision and the judges gave differing reasons for their decision. Lord Hutton dissented on this point stating that "it is not unprincipled to have regard to practical realities where the issue relates to knowledge in a drugs case". Lord Steyn argued for outlawing reverse burdens where the defence bears directly on the moral blameworthiness of the defendant. An important factor in this case was the seriousness of the offence charged. See the discussion above on the nature of a criminal charge for the preliminary conditions for the application of the presumption of innocence. *McIntosh, Benjafield* and *Phillips* all lead to the conclusion that the presumption of innocence guaranteed in Article 6(2) is a specific example of the more general obligation of fair trial rights enshrined in Article 6(1).

Legal Aid and Equality of Arms

Key Principle: Everyone charged with a criminal offence has the right to defend himself in person or through legal assistance of his own choosing, or if he had not sufficient means to pay for legal assistance to be given it free when the interests of justice so require.

Benham v. U.K.
The applicant was imprisoned for non-payment of the community charge after a hearing in the magistrates' court under its civil jurisdiction. The proceedings were classified as civil and he was denied legal aid. He alleged violations of Articles 5 and 6.

Held: (ECtHR) Since the defendant's liberty was at stake the interests of justice required that the matter be treated as a criminal charge. Legal representation should have been allowed. [1996] 22 E.H.R.R. 293

Murray v. U.K.
For facts see above.

Held: (ECtHR) In view of the fact that remaining silent had serious consequences at the trial the pressure on the defendant to speak to the police was sufficiently great to warrant the presence of a lawyer. The failure to secure the solicitor's presence therefore was a breach of Article 6(3). (1996) 22 E.H.R.R. 29

Commentary
The importance of legal professional privilege has been acknowledged. In *S v. Switzerland* the ECtHR (1992) 14 E.H.R.R. 670 held that "free communication between a lawyer and his detained client is a fundamental right which is essential in a democratic society above all in the most serious cases." In *Campbell and Fell v. U.K.* (1984) 7 E.H.R.R. 165 the court accepted however that although in principle those consultations should be conducted in private there were exceptional circumstances where this need not be so, for example if there were reasonable grounds to suspect counsel of abusing his professional position, perhaps by colluding with his client to destroy evidence. As a result of *Murray v. U.K.* the law was amended so that inferences from silence when questioned can be drawn only if the accused has been offered an opportunity to consult a solicitor (see CJPOA 1994, sections 34–37 as amended by the Youth Justice and Criminal Evidence Act 1999). As a result of this decision the Youth Justice and Criminal Evidence Act 1999 has amended the CJPOA to impose an additional condition that if the defendant was at an authorised place of detention at the time of his failure or refusal, no inference may be drawn unless he was afforded an opportunity to consult a solicitor before the request was made. The cases illustrate that the requirement of the availability of legal aid will vary according to the

complexity of issues for the particular defendant and the severity of the penalty. Legal aid is not available for some criminal charges under English law and it may be that this will lead to successful claims under Article 6.

Key Principle: **A system of fixed fees for defendants' solicitors in legal aid cases does not breach the principle of equality of arms.**

McLean and McLean v. Procurator Fiscal Fort William
Under the Criminal Legal Aid (Fixed Payments) (Scotland) Regulations 1999 (S.I. 1999/491) solicitors were paid fixed sums for cases no matter what the complexity. In the instant case the expenditure incurred exceeded the fee payable. It was argued that breached the principle of equality of arms since the prosecution had no such limits.

Held: (PC) There was no breach of Article 6. Article 6 guaranteed the right to effective representation and the question was whether the system was institutionally incapable of providing adequate representation rather than what people were paid. While the regulations were not likely to cause a breach in this case, there was a real likelihood that they could do so in another serious case. However fixed fees were not wrong in principle. [2001] U.K.H.R.R. 793

Commentary
The Privy Council left open the possibility of a claim being brought if the regulations were not changed. The principle of equality of arms runs throughout Article 6 and particularly impact on the rights of legal representation and the right to examine witnesses.

Right to Question Witnesses

Key Principle: **Since everyone charged with a criminal offence has the right to examine or have examined witnesses** against him and to obtain the attendance and examination of witnesses on his behalf under the same conditions as witnesses against him the testimony of anonymous witnesses may generally not be admitted.

Saidi v. France
The applicant was sentenced to 10 years' imprisonment for drug offences. The case was based on identification evidence of three persons but the applicant was denied any opportunity to confront the witnesses.

Held: (ECtHR) As a rule the defendant should be given an adequate and proper opportunity to challenge and question a witness against him whether the witness was making his statement out of court or at a later stage of the proceedings. The court was aware of the difficulties of the fight against drug trafficking, in particular with regard to obtaining and producing evidence, and of the ravages caused to society by the drug problem but such considerations could not justify restricting the rights of the defence to such an extent. (1994) 17 E.H.R.R. 251

Doorson v. Netherlands
The applicant was convicted of drug trafficking on the evidence of witnesses who had not been heard in his presence and whom he had not been given an opportunity to question. He complained of violation of Articles 6(1) and (3)(d).

Held: (ECtHR) Use of anonymous witnesses was not in all circumstances compatible with the Convention. While Article 6 does not refer explicitly to the protection of the interests of witnesses and victims, these are protected by other articles of the Convention. The Court of Appeal was entitled to consider that the applicant's interests were outweighed by the need to insure the safety of witnesses. The court had not based its finding solely on the anonymous evidence. (1996) 22 E.H.R.R. 330

Commentary
If witnesses are potentially vulnerable to attack from defendants then written submissions may be acceptable. In *Doorson* the court observed that "principles of a fair trial also require that in appropriate cases the interests of a defendant are balanced against those of witnesses or victims, called upon to testify". The potential clash between these interests has arisen on a number of issues,

particularly those relating to rape trials. Under section 41 of the Youth Justice and Criminal Evidence Act 1999 defendants are not allowed to cross-examine an alleged victim in person. English criminal procedure does not normally allow pre-trial hearings without the defendant being present so that the safeguard present in *Doorson* is not available. It is arguable that the admissibility of hearsay evidence under the Criminal Justice Act 1988 may violate Article 6 in denying the defendant the right to cross examine. However as regards hearsay evidence admitted for the prosecution the Court of Appeal considered in *R. v. Gokal* (1997) 2 Cr.App.R. 266 that there had been no breach of Article 6 in admitting documentary hearsay because the whole basis of section 26 of the Criminal Justice Act 1988 is to assess the interests of justice by referring to the risk of unfairness to the accused (See also *Trivedi v. U.K.* [1997] E.H.R.L.R. 521).

Fairness of Whole Proceedings

Key Principle: **The taking of evidence is governed primarily by the rules of domestic law and compliance with the European Convention on Human Rights is judged by whether the proceedings in their entirety, including the way in which evidence was taken, were fair.**

Blastland v. U.K.
The applicant had been convicted of murder and buggery of a boy. He denied murder but stated that he had attempted buggery and run when he had seen another man M near the scene. He sought to adduce evidence of witnesses that M had told them a boy had been murdered before the body had been discovered. The trial judge refused to allow this evidence and the House of Lords had decided that the evidence had been rightly excluded. It was untested hearsay and would be treated as having probative force it did not possess. He claimed a violation of Article 6.

Held: (Commission) Application failed. The accused's right to a fair trial was protected procedurally since he was entitled in theory to call M as a witness. [1987] 10 E.H.R.R. 528

Commentary
This is a disturbing case since the defendant had been denied the right to adduce evidence of an implied admission by a third party

of guilt. The Commission however felt that as a whole the rule against the admissibility of hearsay evidence did not violate Article 6. Since the defendant in this case had the right to challenge the ruling it could not be said that there was no "equality of arms". If this had not been so the Strasbourg Court might have come to a different decision. In *Vidal v. Belgium* (1992, unpublished) the court upheld the defendant's complaint that he had not had a fair trial where the Brussels Court of Appeal had refused to allow the defendant to call possibly relevant defence evidence because they had given no reason for their refusal. It is possible that the rule against hearsay evidence may be subject to challenge under the HRA. Article 6(3)(d) does not apply to the defence in the same way as to the prosecution so it is possible to argue that hearsay evidence which the prosecution could not adduce should be excluded if tendered by the defence. English law does not differentiate between defence and prosecution evidence in relation to hearsay. Thus the exclusion of cogent exculpatory evidence could constitute a violation of the right to a fair trial. However where there are a number of defendants the exercise by one defendant of a right to put in hearsay evidence might be fair under the Convention from that defendant's point of view and yet be unfair as against another defendant.

Key Principle: **A breach of the fair trial guarantees under the ECHR will almost always lead to the trial being unfair and any conviction overturned on appeal.**

R. v. Togher, Doran, Parsons

The applicants pleaded guilty to offences of drug dealing arising from seizures by the authorities of cocaine in Madrid. They were convicted. Prior to this they had been convicted of drug offences at Frugal. This latter conviction was appealed and a retrial ordered. At the retrial the judge ordered a stay of proceedings because the prosecution had, by means which were arguably unlawful, deprived the defence of its strategic ability to challenge the integrity of the prosecution case. It was not disputed that the separation of the Madrid and Frugal indictments had been because of case management considerations and the defendants argued that the trial judge's ruling in the retrial should have applied to the Madrid indictment and they should not have been required to plead.

Held: (CA) An appeal against conviction where there had been a guilty plea could be allowed if the proceedings had been an abuse of process such that it would be inconsistent with the due administration of justice to allow the plea to stand. On the facts the failures on the part of the prosecution did not amount to the category of misconduct which had to exist before it was right to stay a prosecution. The defendants were only unaware of material which could but for their pleas have been used in order to attack the credibility of the prosecution witnesses. *The Times*, November 21, 2000

Commentary
Togher has been endorsed by the House of Lords in *R. v. Forbes* [2001] 2 W.L.R. 1. It is one of a number of cases where the court has considered the effect of a breach of the ECHR on the safety of convictions. The problem is acute when there is factual evidence of the truth of the conviction but that the integrity of the process is flawed. An earlier Court of Appeal decision, *R. v. Chalkley*, had adopted a narrow approach to this, holding that in cases of guilty pleas the Court of Appeal should concentrate on the reliability of the verdict. This Court of Appeal considered in *Togher* that now the ECHR was part of domestic law it should follow the broader approach of the ECtHR in *Condron v. U.K.* "The question whether the rights of the defence guaranteed to an accused under Article 6 of the Convention were secured in any given case cannot be assimilated to a finding that his conviction was safe in the absence of any inquiry into the issue of fairness." As a matter of first principles the Court of Appeal did not consider that either the use of the word "unsafe" in the legislation or the previous cases compelled an approach which did not correspond with that of the ECtHR. It follows that a finding of unfairness should lead to a conviction being unsafe. An illustration of the effect of this new approach is seen in *Rowe* where eventually the Court of Appeal decided it had no choice but to overturn the convictions. See also *R. v. Williams The Times* March 30, 2001 where the Court of Appeal considered that a breach of Article 6(2) would not automatically mean that a conviction was unsafe.

Unlawfully or Improperly Obtained Evidence

Key Principle: **There is no rule that requires that illegally or improperly obtained evidence should be excluded from a trial.**

Exclusion is a matter of discretion for the trial judge based on the effect on fairness to the proceedings.

Khan v. U.K.

The applicant had been convicted of involvement in importing heroin. The evidence against him came from an electronic listening device installed by police in a private house he visited. He claimed violations of Articles 6 and 8.

Held: (ECtHR) The evidence had been obtained in violation of Article 8 but it had not been unlawful in the sense of being contrary to domestic criminal law. The authenticity of the recordings was not in question only their admissibility. Since the domestic courts could exercise discretion whether or not to admit such evidence and had concluded its admission would not affect the fairness of the trial there was no breach of Article 6. (2000) 8 B.H.R.C. 310

Commentary

The court found a breach of Articles 8 and 12 since there was no legal basis and thus no redress for the invasion of privacy (see p. 131.) Subsequently such covert operations have been placed on a statutory footing in the Regulation of Investigatory Powers Act 2000. If the communication falls outside the statute intercept evidence is generally admissible. In *R. v. P* [2001] 2 W.L.R. 463 the House of Lords upheld a judge's ruling that telephone intercept evidence lawfully acquired by the authorities in a foreign jurisdiction could be used at trial. Deriving support from *Khan v. U.K.*, the House rejected a claim that Article 8 inevitably demanded the exclusion of intercept evidence not covered by the 2000 Act. In *Edwards v. U.K.* (1993) 15 E.H.R.R. 417 the court had stated that the right to a fair trial extends not merely to the trial but also to pre-trial procedures. Clearly however the mere fact that the evidence had been obtained illegally does not render the trial unfair. The Strasbourg Court has expressed itself willing to leave questions of the admissibility of evidence to national rules and discretion. For an example of a case where the House of Lords has stated that unlawfully obtained intercept evidence was wrongly admitted at trial see *R. v. Sargent* [2001] 3 W.L.R. 992. Its admission in this instance had rendered a conviction unsafe.

Attorney-General's Reference (No. 3 of 1999)

Under section 64(1) of the PACE 1984 a sample taken from a suspect during the investigation of an offence must be destroyed if that person is "cleared" of that offence and according to section 64(3B) such sample "shall not be used in evidence against that person . . . or for the purposes of any investigation of an offence". In two cases, one involving murder and one rape, the Crown had put forward as part of its case DNA evidence collected during other investigations which had both led to the defendants being acquitted. The Court of Appeal had declared that section 64 was mandatory and such evidence was inadmissible. The Court of Appeal at the request of the Attorney-General referred a question for the opinion of the House of Lords as to whether in such circumstances a judge had a discretion to the relevant evidence notwithstanding the terms of section 64(3B).

Held: (HL) Decision of Court of Appeal reversed. Whereas section 64(3B) of the 1984 Act made express prohibition against the use of a DNA sample which should have been destroyed, section 64(3B) in prohibiting the use of an unlawfully retained sample for the purposes of any investigation did not amount to a mandatory exclusion of evidence obtained as a result of a failure to comply with the prohibition. It should be read along with section 78 which left the question of its admissibility to the discretion of the trial judge. A decision by a judge in the exercise of his discretion to admit such evidence would not breach Articles 8 or 6 of the Convention. The information obtained as a result of the failure to destroy the DNA sample ought not to have been rendered inadmissible. [2001] 2 A.C. 91

Commentary
Lord Steyn referred specifically to the principle of fairness for all sides and reasoned that a consideration of the public interest reinforced his interpretation of the application of section 78. With regard to the argument that Article 8 of the ECHR required the interpretation which the Court of Appeal had come to, he said that "the interpretation was in accordance with law" as judicial discretion under section 78 governed admissibility. The interference was plainly necessary in a democratic society to ensure the investigation and prosecution of serious crime. Lord Steyn pointed out: "respect for the privacy of defendants is not the only value at stake. . . . There must be fairness to all sides. In a criminal case this requires the court to consider a triangulation of interests. It involves taking into account the position of the accused, the victim and his or her family and the public. In my view the austere interpretation which the Court of Appeal adopted. . . produces

results which are contrary to good sense." It has been observed
that this was indeed a sensible decision. It is of interest that in *R. v.
Z* [2000] 2 A.C. 483 the House of Lords held that acquittals are
not to be treated as findings of innocence.

Entrapment

Key Principle: **In entrapment cases the ultimate question was
whether the fairness of the proceedings would be adversely
affected by admitting the evidence of the agent provocateur or
evidence which was available as the result of his action or
activities.**

Teixeira de Castro v. Portugal 1999
Two plain clothes police officers had asked a known petty drug
trafficker to obtain heroin. He mentioned the name of the
applicant who eventually obtained packets of the drug for the
undercover officers. The applicant was arrested, charged and
convicted. He claimed breaches of Articles 3, 6 and 8. He
claimed that the officers had engaged in immoral conduct since
he had supplied the drug solely at the officers' request. They
had not been carrying out drug trafficking searches pursuant to
a court order.

Held: (ECtHR) There was a violation of Article 6 and it was
not necessary to consider violations of Articles 3 and 8. The
officers had instigated and incited the offence and there was
nothing to suggest that but for their intervention it would have
been committed. The applicant had been denied the right to a
fair trial. [1999] 28 E.H.R.R. 101

R. v. Shannon 2001
The defendant was convicted of supplying drugs to a journalist
posing as an Arab sheikh, part of a stratagem to obtain evidence
of drug offences against him. The judge refused an application
to exclude the evidence as unfairly obtained.

Held: (CA) Appeal against conviction dismissed. There was no
general rule requiring a court on grounds of fundamental
fairness not to entertain a prosecution in all cases of incitement
or instigation by an agent provocateur regardless of whether the

trial as a whole could be fair in the procedural sense. The judge found correctly in that the evidence fell short of establishing actual incitement or instigation of the offences and in any event the admission of the evidence would not have an adverse effect on the procedural fairness of the trial. [2001] 1 W.L.R. 51

Commentary

The Court of Appeal referred to *Teixeira de Castro v. Portugal* and considered that the end result of that case, couched as it was in terms of incitement and causation, was not necessarily at odds with English law. It considered that the approach of the Strasbourg Court was not inconsistent with the approach in *R. v. Smurthwaite*, [1994] 1 All E.R. 898 namely that the evidence would be open to exclusion if the incitement had caused the offence.

Key Principle: **In assessing whether to exclude evidence or stay criminal proceedings in cases of entrapment the requirements of Article 6 of the ECHR are compatible with section 78 of the PACE and the common law.**

R. v. Looseley; Attorney-General's reference (No. 3 of 2000)

An undercover police officer who had been given the defendant's name as a potential source of drugs, arranged with him to exchange heroin for money. The defendant was charged with supplying or being concerned in supplying to another a class A controlled drug, contrary to section 4 of the Misuse of Drugs Act 1971. The trial judge refused a preliminary request to exclude evidence or stay proceedings. The defendant pleaded guilty. In a separate case two undercover police officers who offered contraband cigarettes for sale at a housing estate were introduced to the accused as a potential buyer. They sold him cigarettes and asked if he could get them heroin, a request to which he agreed and complied after initial hesitation. He was charged with supplying heroin. The trial judge stayed the proceedings on the ground that the police had incited the commission of the offence and that otherwise the accused would be denied his right to a fair hearing under Article 6(1) of the ECHR. The stay was lifted, the prosecution offered no evidence and the accused was acquitted. The Attorney-General referred for the opinion of the Court of Appeal the question whether in cases of entrapment the judicial discretion conferred by section

78 of PACE and the power to stay proceedings as an abuse of
process had been modified by Article 6(1) of the ECHR. The
Court of Appeal held it had not and that the trial judge had
been wrong to stay the proceedings. The defendant in the first
case appealed and the reference was made from the Court of
Appeal in the second.

Held: (HL) The court must in such cases balance the need to
uphold the rule of law by convicting and punishing those who
committed crimes with the need to prevent law enforcement
agencies acting in a way which offended ordinary notions of
fairness. The House distinguished between entrapment which
might lead to exclusion of evidence and entrapment which will
lead to a stay of prosecution. There is not one simple test. The
court must ask the central question which was whether the
actions of the police were so seriously improper as to bring the
administration of justice into disrepute. If there has been an
abuse of State power, then the appropriate remedy is a stay of
the indictment, rather than exclusion of the evidence under
section 78 of the PACE. The appeal of the defendant in the first
case was dismissed since the undercover officer did no more
than present himself as an ordinary customer to an active drug
dealer and there was nothing in the officer's conduct which
constituted incitement. In the second case on the facts the trial
judge had been entitled to stay the proceedings on the ground
that the officers had instigated the offence by offering induce-
ments which would not ordinarily be associated with the
commission of that offence. The decision of the Court of Appeal
was reversed in part. [2001] 1 W.L.R. 2060

Commentary
The House stated that the principle to be applied was that it would
be unfair and an abuse of process if a person had been lured,
incited or pressurised into committing a crime which he would not
otherwise have committed but that it would not be objectionable if
a law enforcement officer, behaving as an ordinary member of the
public, gave a person an unexceptional opportunity to commit a
crime and that person freely took advantage of the opportunity.
The judgment demonstrated strong judicial recognition of the
dangers of excessive police behaviour in cases of entrapment and
the need for the courts to protect citizens. Following this judgment
the focus of the court's approach must be on an objective
assessment of the conduct of the police rather than the predisposi-
tion of the defendant. Thus, for example, the defendant's criminal

record is unlikely to be relevant. Lord Nicholls specifically recognised that *R. v. Sang* [1980] A.C. 402 had been "overtaken" by statute and case law. Lord Hoffman stressed the importance of the "protection of the integrity of the criminal justice system". Their Lordships considered that their judgment was compatible with *Teixeira de Castro v. Portugal.* It it did not follow from *Teixeira* that taking any active steps, such as offering to buy drugs, necessarily amounts to "incitement". The law was and is that entrapment is not a defence *per se.* Lord Nicholls stated that if there has been entrapment, then even where there is other evidence, the abuse of State power is such that the case should be stopped entirely by means of a stay. Among the factors to be considered will be the following: the nature of the offence; the factual basis for the police carrying out the operation; the degree and extent of the police inducement. The former test of whether the offender was predisposed to commit such an offence was not appropriate.

Disclosure of Evidence

Key Principle: **Failure by the prosecution to disclose documents to the defence may impair the fairness of the proceedings.**

Rowe and Davis v. U.K. 2000
The appellants had been convicted of murder. They contended that their convictions were obtained in violation of Article 6 since they were based on unreliable evidence from witnesses who had vindictive motives for giving evidence, were police informers or had obtained rewards. The trial judge had accepted a prosecution request to not disclose documents to the defence and had not reviewed the documents; the Court of Appeal had reviewed them and refused disclosure.

Held: (ECtHR) The applicants had been denied a fair trial and the Court of Appeal had not been able to remedy the defect of the non inspection of the documents by the trial judge. The trial judge was best placed to decide whether non disclosure of public interest immunity evidence would be unfairly prejudicial to the defence. A fundamental principle of a fair trial in the adversarial system was that there was equality of arms. There

may be occasions when documents were not made available to
the defence but this had to be "strictly necessary".

Commentary

The court referred approvingly to *R. v. Ward* [1993] 1 W.L.R. 619
in its judgment. The convictions of the appellants were overturned
by the Court of Appeal which held that a conviction may be unsafe
even where there was no doubt about guilt but the trial process
had been "vitiated by serious unfairness or significant legal mis-
direction" (see *R. v. Rowe and Davis, The Times*, July 25, 2000).
By contrast to the ruling in *Rowe et al. v. U.K.*; *Jasper v. U.K.*; *Fitt
v. U.K.* (2000) there was no violation of Article 6(1) since the
defence were notified of the *ex parte* hearing and were allowed to
present their case to the judge. The court observed in the latter
cases that disclosure of relevant evidence is not an absolute right
and that competing interests of national security, protecting witnesses and preserving the secrecy of police investigative methods
have to be balanced against those of the accused. These considerations affect the operation of the doctrine of public interest
immunity. However a more general issue is the disclosure of
prosecution evidence to the defence. It is arguable that the regime
under the Criminal Procedure and Investigations Act 1996,
whereby secondary disclosure is postponed until after a defence
statement, may not be compatible with the Convention. This case
is commonly known as the M25 Case. (For another example of the
same principle see *Atlan v. U.K.* (App. No. 36533/97) June 19,
2001).

No punishment without law

Key Principle: **Article 7 of the ECHR—No punishment without law:**

> "1 No one shall be held guilty of any criminal offence on
>   account of any act or omission which did not constitute a
>   criminal offence under national or international law at the
>   time when it was committed. Nor shall a heavier penalty
>   be imposed than the one that was applicable at the time
>   the criminal offence was committed.
>
> 2 This article shall not prejudice the trial and punishment of
>   any person for any act or omission which, at the time
>   when it was committed, was criminal according to the
>   general principles of law recognised by civilised nations."

Key Principle: **An order which was designed to protect the public rather than inflict punishment did not infringe Article 7.**

Gough v. Chief Constable of Derbyshire

The appellant argued that a football banning order was a violation of Article 7 in that when he committed the relevant act the maximum penalty was 3 years which was later increased to 6. He had been given 6 years.

Held: (CA) The order was not a penalty for the purposes of Article 7 since it was to protect the public at home and abroad from the threat of football violence. Such measures to counter this sickening menace were proportionate. [2001] 3 W.L.R. 1392

Commentary

It was also submitted that the orders were contrary to the free movement of people under E.U. law. The court held that it was possible to derogate from these laws on public policy grounds.

Key Principle: **A strong indication of a regime of punishment will engage Article 7.**

Welch v. U.K.

The applicant was convicted of drug offences. The trial judge imposed a confiscation order under the Drug Trafficking Act 1986 which came into force after the applicant's arrest but before conviction. He claimed this was a violation of Article 7.

Held: (ECtHR) Factors to be taken into account in deciding whether an order was a penalty were: whether the order was imposed after a criminal conviction; its nature and purpose; its characterisation under national law; its severity; and the procedures involved in its making and implementation. In view of the combination of punitive elements there was a violation of Article 7. (1995) 20 E.H.R.R. 247

Commentary

Drug confiscation orders have also been subject to scrutiny under Article 6 (see p. 7). In 1994 the Drug Trafficking Act replaced

the earlier legislation. Confiscation orders are no longer mandatory. Either the prosecution may seek an order or the court of its
own motion may do so.

5. DUE PROCESS AND A FAIR TRIAL IN CIVIL PROCEEDINGS

Key Principle: **Article 5 of the ECHR—Right to liberty and
security:**

> "1 Everyone has the right to liberty and security of person.
> No one shall be deprived of his liberty save in the
> following cases and in accordance with a procedure
> prescribed by law:
> . . .
>
>> (f) the lawful arrest or detention of a person to prevent
>> his effecting an unauthorised entry into the country
>> or of a person against whom action is being taken
>> with a view to deportation or extradition."

Detention of Asylum Seekers

Key Principle: **The detention of asylum seekers awaiting
determination of their applications is both lawful under
domestic law and does not violate the right to liberty under
Article 5.**

R. (Saadi) v. Secretary of State for the Home Department
Four asylum seekers had claimed judicial review of the lawfulness of their temporary detention at Oakington reception centre
after their arrival in the United Kingdom. Oakington had been
established as a reception centre for asylum seekers whose
claims could be decided usually within 10 days of arrival. It was
accepted that none of the claimants presented any risk of
absconding or of otherwise failing to comply with the terms of

temporary admission while their claims for asylum were being processed and the sole reason for their detention was to facilitate the "fast track" disposal of their claims. Collins J. in the administrative court had held that the detention was unlawful under Article 5. The Secretary of State appealed.

Held: (CA) The claimants' detention fell within the express statutory powers of immigration officers. Article 5 allowed detention to prevent an "unauthorised entry into the country". "Unauthorised entry" was an entry which had not be authorised. No disproportionality was demonstrated. Appeal allowed. [2002] 1 W.L.R. 356

Commentary

The court stated that the Convention was a living instrument and when interpreting it and considering the Strasbourg jurisprudence it was necessary to bear in mind that its effect might change in step with changes in the standards applied by Member States. But as a starting point it was sensible to consider the position in 1951 when the Convention was agreed. In accepting Article 5 Member States were not binding themselves to grant aliens unlimited license to enter their territories and enjoy liberty within them. The right of the state to determine whether aliens should enter was a firmly entrenched principle of international law. The exception to the right to liberty in Article 5(1)(f) was intended to preserve the right of Member States to decide whether to allow aliens to enter.

Fair Trial Rights

Key Principle: **Article 6 of the ECHR—Right to a fair trial:**

"1 In the determination of his civil rights and obligations or of any criminal charge against him, everyone is entitled to a fair and public hearing within a reasonable time by an independent and impartial tribunal established by law. Judgment shall be pronounced publicly but the press and public may be excluded from all or part of the trial in the interests of morals, public order or national security in a democratic society, where the interests of juveniles or the protection of the private life of the parties so require, or to the extent strictly necessary in the opinion of the court in special circumstances where publicity would prejudice the interests of justice."

Access to the courts

Key Principle: **The state cannot preclude access to a judicial procedure.**

Golder v. U.K.
A prisoner in Parkhurst was accused by a prison officer of having taken part in a disturbance. The officer later withdrew the allegation and the prisoner petitioned for the right to consult a solicitor with a view to bringing a libel action against the officer. The Home Secretary refused. The applicant claimed his right of access to justice under Article 6 had been denied.

Held: (ECtHR) Article 6(1) contains the right of access to a court and in civil matters "one can scarcely conceive of the rule of law without there being the possibility of having access to a court". The right to institute civil proceedings is one aspect of the right of access to a court. This right was not an absolute and could be subject to limitations. On the facts in this case there was an infringement of Article 6(1). (1979–80) 1 E.H.R.R. 524

Commentary
In its judgment the court demonstrated how it dealt with a new issue coming before it. It looked both at the content of Article 6(1) and its relationship to other Articles, particularly Articles 5(4) and 13, pointing out that "the three provisions do not operate in the same field. The concept of 'civil rights and obligations' is not co-extensive with that of 'rights and freedoms as set forth in this Convention', even if there may be some overlapping". It also referred to theoretical and abstract issues particularly the "rule of law". As a result of this important case the Prison Rules in force then were amended to allow a prisoner to institute proceedings or to consult a solicitor.

Osman v. U.K. 1999
The widow and son of a murder victim sought to sue police who had allegedly ignored warnings in advance of the murder that the killer, a former teacher of the son, was acting dangerously. The applicants were prevented from bringing an action in negligence by a rule of public policy and argued that this was a restriction on their right of access to the courts.

Held: (ECtHR) The failure to allow the applicants' action to proceed to trial was a disproportionate restriction and was a violation of Article 6. The existing rule gave immunity to the police for their acts and omissions during the investigation and suppression of crime. Other public interest considerations should be borne in mind, otherwise there would be no distinction between degrees of negligence or of harm suffered or any consideration of the justice of a particular case. (1999) 29 E.H.R.R. 245.

Commentary

In *Osman* the Strasbourg Court stretched Article 6(1) to include not only procedural guarantees but the availability of a cause of action. The court had to be satisfied that a right did exist under domestic law. Here the civil right was derived from the general tort of negligence. The blanket ban on actions against the police derived from *Hill v. Chief Constable of West Yorkshire Police* was a violation of an individual's right. This was potentially a far reaching decision and its effect was seen for example in *Hall v. Simons* [2000] 3 W.L.R. 543 where the House of Lords removed the immunity in civil suit of advocates. However the Strasbourg Court subsequently appeared to retreat from the robust ruling in *Osman*. In *Z v. U.K.* [2001] ECHR 29392/95 the court stated (at para. 100) that it

> "considers that its reasoning in the *Osman* judgement was based on an understanding of the law of negligence . . . which has to be reviewed in the light of the clarifications subsequently made by the domestic courts and notably the House of Lords. . . . In the present case, the Court is led to the conclusion that the inability of the applicants to sue the local authority flowed not from an immunity but from the applicable principles governing the substantive right of action in domestic law. There was no restriction on access to court of the kind contemplated in the *Ashingdane v. United Kingdom* (1985) judgement."

In *Barrett v. Enfield LBC* [1999] 3 All E.R. 193 the House of Lords had implemented reforms to the tort of negligence. In *Z v. U.K.* the court had found no violation of Article 6 arising from the fact that children who had suffered neglect in local authority care could not sue the authority in negligence. This rule was the application of substantive law principles by the domestic courts and it was not for the ECtHR to rule on the appropriate content of domestic law. See also pp. 17, 35, 54.

Key Principle: **Access to the courts must not be made practically impossible by high court fees.**

R. v. Lord Chancellor, *ex parte* Witham

The Lord Chancellor increased the fees for issuing a writ and abolished exemption from paying fees for litigants in person in receipt of income support. The applicant was an unemployed man in receipt of income support who wished to issue proceedings in person for defamation for which legal aid was not available. He was not able to afford the fees and sought judicial review of the Lord Chancellor's decision.

Held: (DC) Access to the courts was a constitutional right at common law and could be abrogated only by a specific statutory provision in primary legislation. The Lord Chancellor had no power to prescribe fees so as to deny the poor access to the courts and his decision to do so was *ultra vires* and unlawful. [1998] Q.B. 575

Commentary

The judgment of Laws J. contains a full survey of English cases on the common law and rights of access to justice. Laws J. made reference to Article 6 but stated that " the common law provides no lesser protection to the right of access to the Queen's courts than might be vindicated in Strasbourg". See also *R. v. Home Secretary, ex parte Leech* [1994] Q.B. 198

Key Principle: **The right of access to the courts is not an absolute one.**

Ashingdane v. U.K.

The applicant who had been convicted of a criminal offence, was sent to a secure special hospital. The Home Secretary ordered he be transferred to a local psychiatric hospital but this was delayed because of industrial action. Legislation protected the authorities from civil suit for failure to comply with an order as long as there was no allegation of negligence or bad faith. The applicant complained there was a breach of Article 6(2) since he was thus prevented from challenging at law his prolonged detention in a secure hospital.

Held: (ECtHR) Any restrictions on the right of access to the courts must be proportionate and must not restrict or reduce access in such a way that the right itself was impaired. The court accepted that the objective of the legislation was to reduce the risk of unfair harassment of those responsible for these mental patients. This was a legitimate aim and did not "transgress the principle of proportionality". There was thus no violation of Article 6(1). (1985) 7 E.H.R.R. 528

Commentary
There are a number of groups of litigants or would be litigants who are disadvantaged in getting to court at all. These include prisoners, mental patients, bankrupts. *Ashingdane* makes it clear that although the essential right of access to the courts to pursue civil claims must be upheld some procedural limitations are acceptable in these types of cases.

Key Principle: **Limitation periods must be proportionate and pursue a legitimate aim.**

Stubbings v. U.K.
The applicant claimed that she had been abused for a number of years by her adoptive father and his son and that as a result she had suffered severe psychological damage. She only realised the cause when undergoing psychiatric treatment years later. Her claim against the alleged perpetrators was time barred under the Limitation Act 1980. She claimed a breach of Article 6.

Held: (ECtHR) Limitation periods served the legitimate aim of ensuring legal certainty and finality and a six year limitation period was not unduly short. There had been no violation. (1996) 3 E.H.R.R. 213

Commentary
The court recognised that society's attitude to the offence of child sex abuse and its effects on victims might change. It stated: "It is possible that the rules on limitations of actions applying in Member States of the Council of Europe may have to be amended to make special provision for this group of claimants in the near future."

Key Principle: **The right of access to a court extends only to disputes over civil rights and obligations which are recognised under domestic law.**

Fayed v. U.K.
The applicants had acquired ownership of the House of Fraser. The Government appointed two inspectors to investigate the take over and they published a report which was critical of the applicants. The applicants complained that they had no redress in law and there was a violation of Article 6.

Held: (ECtHR) The state had not exceeded its margin of appreciation in limiting the access to a court; there were safeguards in the procedure of investigative inquiry which was not determinative of a civil right or criminal liability. There was no violation of Article 6(1). (1994) 18 E.H.R.R. 393

Commentary
In *Fayed* the court recognised that the protection of public interests was an important factor in the activities of the investigators operating under the Companies Act 1985 and therefore it was important that inspectors were allowed freedom to report with "courage and frankness". The case illustrates also that Article 6(1) does not necessarily apply to official inquiries. The court concluded that there was an important difference between adjudication which was covered by Article 6(1) and investigation which was not. The finding that the applicant was dishonest as a result of the investigation was not a "determination" since it was not "dispositive of anything" in the way of legal rights and duties.

Legal Aid

Key Principle: **Legal aid in civil proceedings may be necessary in order to secure the right of access to a court.**

Airey v. Ireland
For facts see p. 114.

Held: (ECtHR) The Convention was intended to guarantee rights that are not theoretical or illusory but rights that are practical and effective. Legal aid in was required to allow the applicant to pursue her case in view of the complexity of the issues. (1979) 2 E.H.R.R. 305

Commentary
After referring to criminal legal aid in Article 6(3)(c) the court stated "despite the absence of a similar clause for civil litigation, Article 6(1) may sometimes compel the State to provide for the assistance of a lawyer. . .". The court stressed that it did not hold that legal aid must be provided in all civil proceedings. Legal aid was needed only where it was "indispensable for effective access to court either because legal representation was compulsory" or because of the "complexity of the procedure or of the case". It noted in *Winer v. U.K.* (1986) 48 D.R. 154 there was no breach where legal aid was not available for defamation cases. In *Airey* the court commented that simplifying procedures might be one way of ensuring an effective right of access. The case does suggest that the complete absence of legal aid to enable a litigant to press a claim may be an infringement of Article 6. Some commentators have questioned whether the conditional fee system might be regarded as an adequate substitute.

Impartiality and Equality of Arms

Key Principle: **Civil rights and obligations should be determined by an independent and impartial tribunal.**

Starrs and Chalmers v. Procurator Fiscal
The Lord Advocate appointed temporary sheriffs to hear a large proportion of criminal cases in Scotland. It was argued that such an appointment system including lack of security of office and the discretion of the Lord Advocate, was incompatible with the right to a fair trial.

Held: (Court of Session) The appointment of temporary sheriffs under section 11(4) of the Sheriff Courts (Scotland) Act 1971 was incompatible with Article 6(1) as they did not constitute an independent and impartial tribunal. (2000) U.K.H.R.R. 78

Commentary
While the HRA was in force in England from October 2000 it was in effect in Scotland on the devolution of power to the Scottish

Parliament in 1998 and cases in Scotland gave an early indication of the impact of the Act. With regard to impartiality a key requirement is that the tribunal should be independent of the executive. The Lord Advocate controlled appointments and he was also head of the prosecution service. In *Langborger v. Sweden* (1990) 12 E.H.R.R. 416 the court set out the factors which should be considered in determining whether the tribunal was independent. These included the manner of appointment of the members, their term of office, the existence of guarantees against outside pressure, whether the body in question presents an appearance of independence. There should be both lack of actual bias and of the appearance of bias. *Starrs* has implications for the system of judicial appointments throughout the United Kingdom. The court recognised that the fact that the executive appoints judges does not in itself threaten judicial independence but that where a judge is appointed on a temporary basis and his appointment lies at the discretion of the Executive judicial independence may be at risk.

Key Principle: **Decisions by the Secretary of State were not incompatible with Article 6(1) provided they were subject to review by an independent and impartial tribunal.**

R. (Alconbury Developments Ltd) v. Secretary of State for Environment, Transport and the Regions

In three separate planning cases the Secretary of State played a part in deciding whether or not planning permission should be granted. It was argued that the Secretary of State's role was contrary to the right to have their civil rights and obligations determined by an independent and impartial tribunal guaranteed by Article 6(1) of the Convention. The Divisional Court held that the Secretary of State's powers were incompatible with Article 6(1) but that his exercise of those powers was not unlawful because section 6(2) of the HRA applied. The Secretary of State appealed to the House of Lords.

Held: (HL) Although the Secretary of State was not himself an independent and impartial tribunal, decisions taken by him were not incompatible with Article 6(1) if they were subject to review and by an independent and impartial tribunal. The reviewing body did not need full power to redetermine the merits of the decision. It would be undemocratic for the courts to review ministerial policy decisions on their merits. Compatibility with Article 6(1) was ensured by the power of the High Court in judicial review proceedings to review the legality of the decision and the procedures followed. [2001] 2 W.L.R. 1389

Key Principle: **Civil hearings should usually be public ones.**

Campbell and Fell v. U.K.
For facts see p. 66.

Held: There was a no breach of Article 6 in failing to hold the hearing in public since there were sufficient reasons of public order and security justifying the exclusion of the press and public. But there was no justifiable reason why the decision of the board should not have been made public and to this extent there was a violation of Article 6(1). (1984) 7 E.H.R.R. 165

Commentary
Article 6(1) lists grounds under which the press and public may be excluded from all or part of a trial. These are: the interests of morals, public order, national security, where the interests of juveniles or respect for the private life of the parties so require or to the extent strict publicity would prejudice the interests of justice. In *B v. U.K.* and *P v. U.K.* (2001), *The Times*, May 15, 2001 the court made it clear that the right to a public hearing is not absolute and in this case a private hearing was in the interests of the children involved.

Key Principle: **Each party in civil proceedings must be afforded a reasonable opportunity to present his case, including his evidence, under conditions that do not place him at a substantial disadvantage with regard to his opponent.**

McGinley and Egan v. U.K.
The applicants had been refused a war pension. They claimed they suffered medical problems arising from their exposure to high levels of radiation. They complained that the Government had withheld documents which would have helped their claim.

Held: (ECtHR) There was an effective procedure for the determination of claims under the Pension Appeals Tribunal Rules

1981 which the applicants had failed to use. There was no breach of Article 6. (1999) 27 E.H.R.R. 1

Commentary
Although the court rejected the applicants' claim on the facts it emphasised that denial of access to documents which would assist a party's case was a breach of the right to a fair hearing. The court has insisted that the principle of the equality of arms means that proceedings which determine civil rights and obligations should be adversarial (see *Ruiz–Mateos v. Spain* (1993) 16 E.H.R.R. 505). In *McMichael v. U.K.* (1995) 20 E.H.R.R. 205 Article 6(1) was breached where parents in care proceedings were not given full disclosure of documents including social reports.

Reasons

Key Principle: **Domestic courts should give reasons for their judgments.**

Van de Hurk v. Netherlands 1994
The applicant, who owned a cowshed, claimed the procedure under which his claim to extend his milk quota was rejected violated Article 6(1) on three counts. First his case had not been dealt with by an "independent and impartial" tribunal since the Crown and thus the minister could decide that a judgment of the industrial appeals tribunal should not be implemented; secondly he had not been afforded a "fair hearing" and thirdly the tribunal had not sufficiently dealt with the arguments he had advanced in a reasoned judgment.

Held: (ECtHR) Article 6(1) obliges courts to give reasons for their decisions but cannot be understood as requiring a detailed answer to every argument. The court did not find that the judgment of the industrial appeals tribunal was insufficiently reasoned. (1994) 18 E.H.R.R. 481

Commentary
The court did find a violation in the first of the applicant's claims but not in the second. One reason why it is important that reasons be given is so that parties can exercise their rights of appeal. Some civil trials are held in front of a jury who are not required to give reasons.

Costs

Key Principle: **There must be fair rules for allocating costs.**

Robins v. U.K.
The applications arose out of a dispute between the applicants and their neighbours over sewerage. The applicants contended that the costs proceedings after the conclusion of the civil litigation were not concluded in a reasonable time, in violation of Article 6(1).

Held: (ECtHR) The legal costs were incurred during the resolution of the dispute which involved the termination of civil rights and obligations. Article 6(1) was violated in view of the unreasonable delay in dealing with the case. (1997) 26 E.H.R.R. 527

Commentary
The cost proceedings involved the Legal Aid Board and had taken four years to complete. The courts recognised that the state authorities could not be held responsible for the totality of the delays. However the Department of Social Security had been at fault and for a period of 16 months the court authorities had been totally inactive. The Commission had held that costs proceedings after the civil litigation was over were not covered by Article 6(1) but the court disagreed stating that Article 6(1) "requires that all stages of legal proceedings for the determination of . . . Civil rights and obligations, not excluding stages subsequent to judgment on the merits, be resolved within a reasonable time. The ECHR is silent on whether the successful party should be awarded costs. It is implicit in *Robins* that all matters relating to costs should be settled fairly. The court stated in *Grepne v. U.K.* [1990] 66 D.R. 268 that "it is not an unreasonable requirement of civil litigation that the unsuccessful party may have to pay the adversary's costs."

Key Principle: **High security for costs orders do not necessarily infringe Article 6(1).**

Tolstoy Miloslavsky v. U.K.
The applicant had been successfully sued for libel by Lord Aldington whom he had accused in a pamphlet of arranging the perpetration of a major crime. Record damages were awarded

by the jury in the High Court. The applicant wanted to appeal but was prevented from doing so by an order of the Court of Appeal that he pay into court nearly £125,000 within 14 days as security for his opponent's costs. He failed to do so and his appeal was dismissed. He complained that the damages award infringed his freedom of expression and that the security for costs order infringed his right to access to the Court of Appeal.

Held: (EctHR) Although the exceptionally high damages award infringed Article 10 there was no breach of Article 6. (1995) 20 E.H.R.R. 442

Commentary
The court stated that its task was not to "substitute itself for the competent British authorities in determining the most appropriate policy for regulating access to the Court of Appeal in libel cases nor to assess the facts which led the court to adopt one decision rather than another. The court's role is to review under the Convention the decision that those authorities have taken in the exercise of their powers of appreciation." The court stressed that it was here concerned with the appeal stage so its reasoning may not necessarily apply to orders for costs at the trial stage before evidence has been submitted.

Delay

Key Principle: **Delay in concluding civil proceedings may breach Article 6.**

Darnell v. U.K.
The applicant, a consultant microbiologist with the Thames Regional Health Authority, had faced disciplinary hearings and been dismissed in 1984. His dismissal was confirmed two years later by the Secretary of State. The applicant successfully challenged the fairness of the procedure leading to his dismissal in a judicial review. The Secretary of State, having been asked to reconsider, confirmed the dismissal in 1988. Another application for judicial review was refused. In 1990 the industrial tribunal, whose proceedings had been stayed pending the outcome of the

appeals, held the dismissal was not unfair. In 1993 the Employment Appeal Tribunal (EAT) dismissed the appeal. The applicant contended that the period of nine years from his dismissal to the final EAT ruling breached Article 6.

Held: (ECtHR) The long delay between the initial application to the Industrial Tribunal and the EAT ruling was not reasonable. (1991) 69 D.R. 306

Commentary
The court has not applied a strict set of criteria for assessing whether the delay in civil cases is reasonable. A number of factors will be taken into account including the complexity of the case, the importance of the issue for the applicant, and the conduct of the courts and the applicant. Employment disputes are one example where fairness would require a prompt outcome (see *Obermeier v. Germany*).

Employees

Key Principle: **Internal workplace disciplinary hearings do not attract the protection of Article 6.**

Darnell v. U.K.
See above.

Held: (ECtHR) The period which engaged Article 6 did not include the time it took to hear the internal disciplinary hearings. (1991) 69 D.R. 306

Commentary
A number of commentators are sceptical about the potential impact of Article 6 on employment law matters. Professor Hepple has argued that Article 6 adds nothing to the procedural safeguards which exit under the Employment Tribunals Act 1996 for both private and public employees. See also *C v. U.K.* where the Commission noted "whilst internal professional disciplinary proceedings against persons employed in public service may not attract the guarantees of Article 6(1) of the Convention, when a contract of employment, albeit in the public service, permits access to the civil courts to determine the respective civil liabilities of the

parties, the proceedings before the normal courts may usually be said to determine civil rights and obligation within the meaning of Article 6(1) of the Convention." (1987) 54 D.R. 162

Key Principle: **The right to a reputation is a civil right but school exclusion proceedings do not embrace the determination of that right.**

R. (B, T and C) v. Secretary of State for Education and Employment
The applicants had been excluded, expelled from or declined admission to various schools. Their appeals to the schools' independent appeal tribunals were rejected. They sought review of the decisions on the basis that they had a right to a good reputation, that this right was affected by the decisions of the tribunal and that they should be able to protect that civil right in a tribunal which observed the fair trial guarantees of Article 6(1).

Held: (DC) Article 6 did not apply. The issue in the case went to the content of the right to a reputation rather than its definition and so an authoritative definition of such a civil right was not needed. The content of a right to a reputation was "the right to enjoy a fair reputation". The appeal proceedings did not directly decide the reputations of the pupils and Article 6 did not apply to them. *The Times,* June 8, 2001

Commentary
In *Le Compte, Van Leuven and de Meyere v. Belgium* (1982) E.H.R.R. 47 it was held that to gain the protection of Article 6 the hearing must be "directly decisive of the right in question". In deciding the nature of a civil right the court has looked at the character of the right and its classification in domestic law (*Konig v. Germany* (1979–80) 2 E.H.R.R. 170) and also whether there is a uniform European practice (*Feldbrugge v. Netherlands* (1986) 8 E.H.R.R. 425).

Key Principle: **Public law rights are not embraced within the definition of civil rights and so are not protected by Article 6.**

Balfour v. U.K.

A former diplomat challenged his employers' use of PII in proceedings he had taken over his dismissal.

Held: (Commission) Application inadmissible since the applicant was a public official and Article 6(1) did not apply. (1997) E.H.R.L.R. 665

Commentary

One way that Article 6(1) may cover public sector employees is that some public employees may not be categorised as civil servants. In *C v. U.K.* (1987) 54 D.R. 162 a school caretaker was entitled to claim Article 6 protection. The Commission noted: "whilst internal professional disciplinary proceedings against persons employed in public service may not attract the guarantees of Article 6(1) of the Convention, when a contract of employment, albeit in the public service, permits access to the civil courts to determine the respective civil liabilities of the parties, the proceedings before the normal courts may usually be said to determine civil rights and obligation within the meaning of Article 6(1) of the Convention." Proceedings over purely economic issues such as payment of a salary may be covered by Article 6. See also *Vogt v. Germany* (1995) 21 E.H.R.R. 205 where it was held that German schoolteachers were not "members of the administration of the State" and there could be an issue of a civil right relating to freedom of expression in a dismissal case.

Key Principle: **The right not to be discriminated against on grounds of religious belief or political opinion in employment is a civil right within the meaning of Article 6(1).**

Devlin v. U.K.

The applicant, a catholic and a member of the Irish National Foresters, was unsuccessful in his application for a post of administrative assistant with Northern Ireland Civil Service. Following several appeals the Secretary of State for Northern Ireland issued a certificate stating that the reason for refusal of employment was an act "done for the purpose of safeguarding national security and protecting the public". He was refused permission to challenge this by judicial review. He complained that his rights under Article 6(1) were infringed.

Held: (ECtHR) Article 6 was applicable since the discrimination engaged a civil right. The applicant was not outside the protection of Article 6(1) by virtue of the fact that the post he was applying for was a civil service one. The test now laid down (following *Pelligrin v. France*) only excluded from Article 6(1) disputes raised by public servants whose "duties typify the specific activities of the public service in so far as the latter is acting as the depository of public authority responsible for protecting the general interests of the State or other public authorities." October 30, 2001

Commentary
In this significant decision which revisits the decision in *Balfour* the court noted that the post of "administrative assistant" was not a post where it can be said the incumbent is "wielding a portion of the State's sovereign power" so as to exclude Article 6(1) rights. The right to a court was not absolute but any limitation must pursue a legitimate aim and there must be a reasonable relationship of proportionality between the means employed and the aim sought to be achieved. Here there was no independent scrutiny of the facts, and no evidence as to why the applicant was a security risk. Article 6(1) was breached.

Appeals

Key Principle: **A refusal of leave to appeal does not constitute a determination of civil rights and obligations.**

Porter v. U.K.
The applicant claimed that a refusal of leave to appeal by the House of Lords violated Article 6(1).

Held: (Commission) The application was inadmissible since a refusal of leave did not constitute a determination of civil rights and obligations. [1987] 54 D.R. 207

Commentary
This position was reaffirmed by the Commission in *Comninos & National Justice Compania Naviera SA v. U.K.* (1996) 23 E.H.R.R. CD.

6. PRIVACY AND FAMILY LIFE

Key Principle: **Article 8 of the ECHR—Right to respect for private and family life:**

> "1 Everyone has the right to respect for his private and family life, his home and his correspondence.
>
> 2 There shall be no interference by a public authority with the exercise of this right except such as is in accordance with the law and is necessary in a democratic society in the interests of national security, public safety or the economic well-being of the country, for the prevention of disorder or crime, for the protection of health or morals, or for the protection of the rights and freedoms of others."

General

Key Principle: **There is a positive obligation on public authorities to protect the rights in Article 8.**

Johnston v. Ireland

The first applicant's marriage broke down and he went to live with the second applicant. They had a daughter who was the third applicant. Because the Irish constitution did not allow divorce, the first two applicants were unable to marry, so their daughter was illegitimate. They claimed violations of Articles 8, 9, 12 and 14 of the Convention, concerning their inability to marry, the legal status of unmarried couples and the status of illegitimate children.

Held: (ECtHR) Articles 8, 9 and 12 were not violated by the absence of any provision for divorce. The public authorities had not interfered with the applicants' ability to live together. States were not obliged to establish for unmarried couples a status analogous to that of married couples, or a special regime for couples who would marry if there were divorce. Article 8 did however require that the daughter should be placed legally and socially in a position akin to that of a legitimate child. The absence of an appropriate legal regime reflecting the daughter's natural family ties was a breach of Article 8. (1986) 9 E.H.R.R. 203

Airey v. Ireland
The applicant claimed that the absence of a provision for legal aid in civil proceedings for a judicial separation violated her right under Article 6 to a fair hearing for the determination of her civil rights, since it effectively denied her access to the courts. She also said Article 8 had been violated by the state's failure to provide an accessible legal procedure for the determination of rights and obligations in family law.

Held: (ECtHR) Articles 6 and 8 had both been violated. Convention rights were intended to be practical and effective. It was not realistic to expect the applicant to conduct her own case in the High Court. (1979) 2 E.H.R.R. 305

Commentary
It is clear from this case that the state has a duty to protect the quality of a person's private life. In *Costello-Roberts* (see p. 120) the court stated that although in some circumstances there might be a breach of Article 8 arising from physical punishment in a school,

> "having regard to the purpose and aim of the Convention taken as a whole and bearing in mind that the sending of a child to school necessarily involves some degree of interference with his or her private life, the court considers that the treatment complained of by the applicant did not entail adverse effects for his physical or moral integrity sufficient to bring it within the scope of the prohibition contained in Article 8."

Both these cases illustrate that although the ban on divorce was not in itself a breach of the Article, the state had a duty to protect children born out of wedlock. In *Airey* the court declared:

> "Although the object of Article 8 is essentially that of protecting the individual against arbitrary interference by public authorities, it does not merely compel the state to abstain from such interference. In addition to this primarily negative undertaking, there may be positive obligations inherent in an effective respect from private and family life."

Protecting family life also implies the right of divorced parents to have contact with their children. In *Hendricks v. Netherlands* the Commission stated "The right to respect for family life within the meaning of Article 8 of the Convention includes the right of a divorced parent, who is deprived of custody following the break up of marriage, to have access to or contact with his child." The Convention recognises however that the child's interest will be overriding and on occasion this may require curtailing the access of a parent (see *Whitear v. U.K.* (1997) E.H.R.L.R. 291).

Developing Right to Privacy

Key Principle: **The common law does not recognise a tort of privacy.**

Kaye v. Robertson

A newspaper reporter and photographer invaded the hospital room of a television actor when he was recovering from serious head injuries, violating hospital instructions. The actor obtained an injunction requiring the newspaper to refrain from publishing the interview and photographs the journalists had obtained. The newspaper editor and the publisher appealed.

Held: (CA) There was no right of action for breach of a person's privacy. [1991] F.S.R. 62

Commentary

Glidewell L.J. stated: "the fact of the present case are a graphic illustration of the desirability of Parliament considering whether and in what circumstances statutory provision can be made to protect the privacy of individuals." Bingham L.J. stated: "this case none the less highlights, yet again, the failure of both the common law of England and statute to protect in an effective way the personal privacy of individual citizens." But although there was an invasion of privacy the court decided it could do nothing. This case has now to be considered in the light of *Douglas v. Hello!* (see below). The court reviewed the existing law on privacy. Referring to *Kaye v. Robertson* Brooke L.J. stated that in contrast to the uncompromising position of the Court of Appeal in that case "both academic commentary and extra-judicial commentary by judges over the last 10 years have suggested from time to time that a development of the present frontiers of the breach of confidence action could fill the gap in English law which is filled by privacy law in other countries". This commentary was given a boost recently by the decision of the European Commission of Human Rights in *Earl Spencer v. U.K.* (1998) 25 E.H.R.R. CD 105, and by the coming into force of the HRA 1998. Sedley L.J. concluded that the Q.C. for the actors "has a powerfully arguable case to advance at trial that his two first named clients have a right to privacy which English law will today recognise and where appropriate, protect". He saw privacy as "a qualified right recognised and protected by English law". Regard had also to be given to Article 10 although this did not have a presumptive priority over other rights. In *Secretary of State for the Home Department v. Wainwright, The Times*, January 4, 2002 the Court of Appeal held that since at common law there was no tort of invasion of privacy and because the conduct complained of occurred before the coming into force of the HRA the Act did not apply to introduce a right of privacy retrospectively.

Key Principle: **There is no free-standing right to privacy in English law but such a right may exist if there is a pre-existing legal relationship including contract.**

Douglas v. Hello!

Two Hollywood stars, Michael Douglas and Catherine Zeta-Jones, gave exclusive publication rights in their wedding pictures to *OK!*, a celebrity magazine, retaining a veto over publication of particular photographs. All photography other than by the magazine's own photographer was banned: guests were searched for cameras on arrival, and the couple's employees signed undertakings that they would not take pictures at the wedding. Despite these precautions, photographs were taken surreptitiously at the wedding, and it came to the couple's notice that *Hello!*, a rival celebrity magazine, planned to publish them. It was not clear whether the photographs had been taken by a guest, an employee or an intruder. The claimants obtained an injunction to prevent the publication of the photographs pending trial of an action against *Hello!*, who then appealed.

Held: (CA) If the photographs had been taken by a guest or an employee, *Hello!* might rely on the existing law of confidence on the basis that the photographer had either acted (if an employee) in breach of contract, or (if a guest) in breach of confidence. However if the photographs had been taken by an intruder who was not under an obligation of confidence towards the couple, there was no relationship of trust on which the existing law could bite. In those circumstances the law recognised that it had to protect not only those whose trust had been abused, but also those whose personal lives were subjected to unwarranted intrusion. Sedley L.J. said the law no longer required the construction of an artificial relationship of confidentiality between intruder and victim. Privacy itself could be acknowledged as a legal principle drawn from the fundamental value of personal autonomy. In this particular case the court discharged the injunction against *Hello!*, on the basis that the judge who had granted to the injunction had failed to give his reasons. The case is also important because it establishes that the provision in Article 10(2) permitting restriction of the right of freedom of expression "for the protection of the reputation or rights of others" is to be given as much weight as the substantive right itself in deciding whether to order an injunction limiting freedom of expression. [2001] 2 W.L.R. 992 (CA)

Commentary

The court also considered section 12 of the HRA (see p. 161) which prohibits prior restraint unless the claimant establishes a strong case that the restraint is justified. The court treated it as a balancing mechanism between existing codes of practice on privacy and freedom of the press. Breach of the Press Complaints Commission code was likely, Brooke L.J. said, to result in the grant of an injunction since the claimant's rights under Article 10(2) would then "trump" the publication's right to freedom of expression. The court extended the existing law on confidentiality to situations where the party that was intruding had no relationship of trust or confidence with the claimant. The court took the view that "a development of the present frontiers of a breach of confidence action could fill the gap in English law which is filled by privacy law in other developed countries." But it stopped short of creating a new cause of action which would have meant interpreting the HRA to have horizontal effect. In *A v. B and C Plc, The Times*, March 13, 2002 the Court of Appeal set aside an injunction granted by Jack J. restraining a Sunday newspaper from naming a footballer, married with a family, who had sex with two women in one session. The story had been sold to the newspaper by one of the women. Jack J. had held that the law of confidentiality could apply to sexual relationships regardless of the existence of an express agreement to treat the matters as confidential. There was no public interest in the publication of the articles and the information they contained. The appeal court, however, held that a public figure should recognise that his actions would be closely scrutinised by the media whether or not he had courted publicity. The courts should not act as censors and arbiters of taste. The judge had ignored the importance of a free press. He should not have assumed that it was in the interests of the footballer's wife to be kept in ignorance and he had been wrong to say there was no element of public interest in the disclosure, since the public and the media would inevitably be interested in the doings of a well-known footballer. An injunction would be an unjustified infringement of press freedom. It has been noted that there is now an emergent "right of celebrity" (see *The Times Law*, February 5, 2002, p. 7) with the courts affording greater protection to public figures than the voluntary Press Complaints Commission.

Key Principle: **The law of confidence could, exceptionally, be extended to cover information as to the identity or whereabouts of individuals where its disclosure would put them at risk of serious injury or death.**

Venables v. News Group Newspapers Ltd
Jon Venables and Robert Thompson, the killers of two-year-old James Bulger, were sentenced to be detained at Her Majesty's pleasure. They were aged 11 when they committed the crime, and when they reached 18 became eligible for parole. The mother of their victim headed an influential campaign against the grant of parole, and several newspapers wished to publish up-to-date photographs of the boys and details of their present whereabouts. Thompson and Venables sought a continuing injunction against such publication on the basis that injunctions were necessary to protect their rights of confidentiality and their rights to life and freedom from persecution and harassment under the Convention.

Held: (Fam. Div.) The ECHR did not give rise in private law proceedings to a free-standing cause of action based on Convention rights but the court as a public authority was obliged to act compatibly with Convention rights in adjudicating on common law causes of action, and had by section 12(4) of the HRA to give direct effect to the right to freedom of expression under Article 10. Freedom of the media could be restricted only if the need for restrictions was such that they were in accordance with the law, necessary in a democratic society and proportionate to the legitimate aim pursued. The law of confidentiality could extend to cover information about the identity and whereabouts of people in circumstances where publication could put their lives at risk. The injunctions were necessary to protect the applicants against the "real and strong possibility" of physical harm or death. Injunction granted against the whole world to stop publication of the identity and whereabouts of the claimants. [2001] 2 W.L.R. 1038

Commentary

The court was here applying *Douglas v. Hello! Ltd.* These cases illustrate that a new right is developing out of existing law. Butler-Sloss P. referred to the rights of the boys under Articles 2 and 3 as well as 8 and stated:

> "under the umbrella of confidentiality there will be information which may require a special quality of protection. In the present case the reason for advancing that special quality is that, if the information was published, the publication would be likely to lead to grave and possibly fatal consequences. In my judgement, the court does have the jurisdiction, in exceptional cases, to extend the protection of confidentiality even to impose restrictions on the press, where not to do so would be likely to lead to serious physical injury, or to death, of the person seeking that confidentiality and there is no other way to protect the applicant other than by seeking relief from the court."

It must be emphasised that this case was a particularly extreme example because the invasion of privacy might lead to threats to the lives of the boys. This is another case in which legal concepts of confidentiality have been stretched to the limit to impose restraint on the media. It demonstrates the judiciary's considerable power and discretion within the new regime brought about by the HRA. See also *Re A (Children, Conjoined Twins: Surgical Separation)* [2001] 2 W.L.R. 480. (See also p. 162.)

Physical Integrity

Key Principle: **Article 8 may offer protection for physical integrity beyond that of Article 3.**

Costello-Roberts v. U.K.
The applicant had been beaten as a punishment at an independent boarding school. Violations of Articles 3, 8 and 13 were alleged.

Held: (ECtHR) The treatment did not entail adverse effects for physical or moral integrity sufficient to bring it within the scope of the prohibition in Articles, 3 or 8. (1993) 19 E.H.R.R. 112

Commentary
The court accepted that there might be circumstances where Article 8 offered protection beyond that of Article 3 in relation to physical assault. (See also pp. 31, 53, 114).

Privacy at Work

Key Principle: **Individuals have a right to "private life" at work.**

Niemietz v. Germany
Police searched the premises of a lawyer seeking information which would reveal the identity and possible whereabouts of a suspect. The lawyer complained that the search violated his right under Article 8 to respect for his home and correspondence and had impaired the goodwill of his law office and his professional reputation.

Held: (ECtHR) The right to respect for private life included the right to develop relationships with others. Article 8 could not be applied equally to all unless professional and business activities were included in the notions of "home" and "family life". The fact that correspondence examined by the police was of a professional nature did not render Article 8 inapplicable.

Though the interference was prescribed by law and intended to prevent crime it was not necessary in democratic society. (1993) 16 E.H.R.R. 97

Halford v. U.K.
A senior police officer complained that telephone calls made from her office and from her home had been intercepted without warning, in violation of her rights to respect for private life and freedom of expression.

Held: (ECtHR) Telephone calls made from business premises were covered by the notions of private life and correspondence in Article 8. Employees making calls on an internal telephone system operated by their employer should have a reasonable expectation of privacy. Since domestic law did not regulate the interception of calls on an internal system the interception was not "in accordance with the law", as Article 8 required. There was insufficient evidence to determine whether or not the claimant's home phone had been tapped. (1997) 24 E.H.R.R. 523

Commentary
As a result of the latter case the Government introduced a statutory procedure to regulate interception of internal telecommunications systems, the Regulation of Investigatory Powers Act 2000 which affects the privacy of employees. The Government may now argue that interference is in accordance with the law although it is still open to the courts to declare the statute incompatible with the Convention.

Family life

Key Principle: **Legislation which discriminates against children born outside marriage is a violation of the right to respect for family life.**

Marckx v. Belgium
A woman and her young daughter complained that Belgian illegitimacy law violated Article 8 and other provisions of the Convention because it required a formal act of recognition to establish maternal affiliation and limited the mother's capacity to give or bequeath and the child's capacity to take or inherit property.

Held: (ECtHR) The legislation failed to respect the applicants' family life contrary to Article 8 and amounted to discrimination under Article 14 because there was no objective and reasonable justification for the different treatment of legitimacy and illegitimacy. (1979) 2 E.H.R.R. 330

Commentary

In this case the court recognised that the concept of a family should be a broadly interpreted one and one which should reflect changing social views. It stated that family life encompasses "at least ties between near relatives, for instance those between grandparents and grandchildren", since such relatives play a considerable part in family life.

Key Principle: **The rights of parents whose children have been removed from the home by a public authority must be protected.**

W v. U.K.

The applicant complained that his access to his child in care had been terminated without due process. He had no viable remedy against the decision to terminate access and some of the proceedings had been over-long.

Held: (ECtHR) The natural family relationship was not terminated when the child was taken into care, so decisions restricting access to the child were interferences with rights under Article 8 and required to be justified. Though the authorities must be allowed some discretion, the need for protection against arbitrary interference was even greater, so it was open to the court to review it. The parents had not been involved in the process to a degree sufficient to provide them with the means of protecting their interests. (1988) 10 E.H.R.R. 29

Responsibilities of public authorities

Key Principle: **State agencies concerned with the welfare of families must consider the rights of individuals in their charge and involve them in any decision-making process.**

TP and KM v. U.K.
A local authority suspected that a child to whom it owed duties under the Child Care Act 1980 was being abused. The child took part in a video interview stating that she had been sexually abused by a man with the same name as her mother's boyfriend but not the boyfriend. The authority placed the child in a place of safety. One year later the mother saw the video. The mother alleged that the delay in providing the video was a breach of Article 8 since as a result the mother had not been able to take part in a meaningful way in the decisions over the child.

Held: (ECtHR) There was a breach of Article 8 and a failure to respect family life. The question whether to disclose the video should have been determined promptly to allow the applicant an effective opportunity to deal with the allegations that her daughter could not be returned safely to her care. App. No. 28945/95

Commentary
For the case's application to Article 6, along with *Z v. U.K.* the law of negligence see p. 99. The case establishes that it is important that family members are involved in cases concerning children.

Abortion

Key Principle: **Legislation which which restricts abortion may be justified.**

Brüggemann and Scheuten v. Federal Republic of Germany
Two women claimed that German law restricting abortion breached their rights under Article 8. The restrictions forced them to use other methods of contraception including renouncing sexual intercourse.

Held: (Commission) Article 8 was engaged since it embraces the right to establish sexual relationships with others. There was no breach because Article 8(1) could not be interpreted to mean that that pregnancy and abortion are solely within the choice of the mother. (1976) 5 D.R. 103

Commentary
The Commission noted that many of the contracting states had laws which set up regulations for the conduct of pregnancy and abortion. In this sensitive area the concept of the margin of appreciation is especially important. For other judgments relating to abortion see also p. 41.

Homosexuality

Key Principle: **Article 8 is violated by a state's prohibition of homosexual acts between consenting adults.**

Dudgeon v. U.K.
The applicant, a resident of Belfast, complained that Northern Ireland law forbidding buggery and gross indecency amounted to unjustified interference with his right to respect for his private life under Article 8. He also claimed to have been discriminated against on sexual grounds and on grounds of his residence since such offences did not exist in the rest of the United Kingdom.

Held: (ECtHR) The prohibition on private homosexual conduct in Northern Ireland was an interference with the right to respect for private life, being unnecessary in a democratic society. The applicant's rights were not breached by the fact that homosexual acts were prohibited between persons under 21 years old. (1982) 4 E.H.R.R. 149

Commentary
The prosecution of sado-masochistic practices was not however a violation in *Laskey, Jaggard and Brown v. U.K.* (1996) 24 E.H.R.R. 1. A key issue is whether the interference with private life is "necessary in a democratic society". Thus in *ADT v. United Kingdom* (2000) App. No. 35765/97 there was a violation of Article 8 in a prosecution for gross indecency of a man who engaged in oral sex and mutual masturbation with four other men. Since the activities were of a non-violent nature the interferences fell outside the narrow margin of appreciation allowed to the state and could not be justified.

Key Principle: **Different ages of consent for heterosexuals and homosexuals is a violation of Article 8 in combination with Article 14.**

Sutherland v. U.K.
The applicant argued that the fixing of the minimum age for lawful homosexual activities at 18 was a violation of his rights to respect for his private life and was a violation of Article 14 since the age of consent was 16 years for heterosexual activities.

Held: (Commission) There was a violation of Articles 8 and 14 despite the fact that the applicant had not been prosecuted or threatened with prosecution. There was no objective and reasonable justification for the maintenance of a higher minimum age of consent to male homosexual rather than to heterosexual acts. (1998) 24 E.H.R.R. CD 22

Commentary
The Commission referred to the words of the court's judgment in *Dudgeon* that decriminalisation does not imply approval. It was not a good ground for maintaining the different age that some of the sectors of the population might otherwise be drawn misguided conclusions.

Key Principle: **Sexuality is a private matter and rules which invaded people's privacy as to their sexuality or which discriminate on the grounds of sexuality may be a violation of Article 8.**

Smith and Grady v. U.K.
Investigation into the applicants' homosexuality resulted in their discharge from the navy in pursuit of a policy of excluding homosexuals from the forces. The applicants complained of degrading treatment and violation of their right to a private life. They also complained that they had no effective remedy.

Held: (ECtHR) Though the interference with the applicants' right to respect for private life was "in accordance with law" and could be said to pursue legitimate national security aims, the perceived problems of allowing homosexuals in the armed forces were not justified because they were founded solely on the negative attitudes of heterosexual personnel. Article 8 had been violated, but the applicants' treatment was not so severe as to constitute degrading treatment. (2000) 29 E.H.R.R. 493

Commentary
The British Government had not produced convincing or weighty reasons to justify the policy on homosexuals in the armed forces. The case also established that employees' rights to privacy were invaded contrary to Article 8 when they were questioned intensively about their sexuality and relationships in cases involving personnel discharged from the armed forces on grounds of homosexuality. See also *Lustig-Prean and Beckett v. U.K.* (2000).

Key Principle: **Homosexual relationships do not fall within the scope of the right to respect for family life ensured by Article 8.**

App. No. 9369/81
The applicants who were in a stable homosexual relationship complained that there was a violation of Articles 8 and 14 in that the United Kingdom immigration authorities had refused to allow the first applicant who was a Malaysian citizen the right to remain with the second applicant who was a British citizen.

Held: (Commission) The complaints were ill-founded since such relationships did not fall within the scope of the right to respect for family life ensured by Article 8. The right to respect for family life does not necessarily include the right to choose the geographical location of that family. (1983) 5 E.H.R.R. 601

Transsexuals and Gender Reassignment

Key Principle: **States have a margin of appreciation with regard to legal recognition of gender reassignment.**

Rees v. U.K.
The applicant was a transsexual who had been registered at birth as female. After medical treatment he changed his name and began living as a male. He complained that the refusal of his application to amend his birth certificate was a breach of Articles 8 and 12.

Held: (ECtHR) The United Kingdom allowed transsexuals to change their names and they could have the official documents issued in their chosen first names and prefix (Mr Mrs Ms or Miss). There was no violation of Articles 8 or 12. (1987) 9 E.H.R.R. 56

Commentary
Under United Kingdom law transsexuals had according to the court "a considerable advantage in comparison with states where all official documents have to conform with the records held by the registry office." The court considered that far from protecting the integrity of private life the registration of civil status to reflect the current sexual status of an individual might have the effect of revealing a change of sexual identity. In the subsequent case of *Cossey* the court referred to the *Rees* judgment with regard to Article 8 and noted that there was a need to keep appropriate legal measures for transsexuals under constant review. There had been no significant scientific development after *Rees*. There was still adversity in European practice and a departure from *Rees* was not necessary to ensure that contemporary positions were reflected in interpreting Article 8. For the position on Article 12 see p. 141.

B v. France
The applicant, registered as a man, was a transsexual who underwent surgery and lived as a woman. She applied to have her birth certificate changed and was refused. She claimed a breach of Article 8.

Held: (ECtHR) The inconvenience suffered by the applicant was sufficiently serious to breach Article 8. A fair balance had not been struck between the general interest and the interest of the applicant. (1993) 16 E.H.R.R. 1

Commentary
These two cases illustrate how the law in this area is undergoing evolution. In *B v. France* the court distinguished *Rees* noting that there were marked differences between France and England with

reference to their law and practice on civil status. In the United Kingdom the status of transsexuals could not be changed without legislation and such a system would have important administrative consequences and would impose new duties on the rest of the population. (See on this *Cossey v. U.K.* p. 141.)

Key Principle: **The state's approach to the legal recognition of gender changes may change with the change of prevailing social attitudes.**

Sheffield and Horsham v. U.K.

The first applicant was married and had a daughter but had been registered at birth as male. She had gender reassignment treatment. On her divorce a judge granted her former spouse's request to have her contact with their daughter terminated. The judge gave as the reason that contact with a transsexual would not be in the child's interest. The second applicant was a British citizen who had also acquired Dutch citizenship. She had been registered at birth as a male and underwent gender reassignment surgery. She had her request to have her birth certificate amended refused. Both applicants claimed violation of Articles 8, 12 and 14.

Held: (ECtHR) There was no violation of Article 8. The applicants had not shown that medical science had settled the question of the aetiology of the condition of transsexualism. It was necessary to keep the area under review in view of changing social views. There were no violations of Articles 12 or 14. (1999) 27 E.H.R.R. 163

Commentary

The court observed that "it continues to be the case that transsexualism raises complex scientific, legal, moral and social issues in respect of which there is no generally shared approach among contracting states." The court acknowledged that this issue is under evolution adding that although in this case the European Court held that there was no breach of the rights granted by Article 8 it did make it clear that the word "respect" does indeed mean that the state has a positive duty to act to protect the private life of its citizens—as opposed to a duty merely to refrain from interference. The state must strike a fair balance between the community and the individual.

Key Principle: **Homosexual and transsexual unions do not constitute a family for the purposes of protection under Article 8.**

X v. U.K.
A female-male transsexual had a long-standing relationship with a woman who had a child by donor insemination. The authorities refused to register the transsexual as the child's father. All three complained that the refusal violated their rights under Articles 8 and 14.

Held: (ECtHR) The three were a *de facto* family to which Article 8 applied. But there was no common European standard concerning the granting of parental rights to transsexuals. The state must be afforded a wide margin of appreciation, given that transsexuality raised complex issues. Article 8 could not be taken to imply an obligation for the state formally to recognise as a child's father a person who was not its biological father. (1997) 24 E.H.R.R. 143

Commentary
The law in this area is undergoing constant evolution. The court has now recognised the need to rectify the civil status of trans-sexuals (see below). While observing however that the social climate had changed since earlier cases on similar issues (see *Rees v. U.K.* p. 127; *Cossey v. U.K.* (1991) 13 E.H.R.R. 622 p. 141) the court noted that the status of transsexuals in the United Kingdom could not be changed without new primary legislation. It had accepted in *Cossey v. U.K.* that the United Kingdom was not required to change its system of registering births since such a system "would have important administrative consequences and would impose new duties on the rest of the population". In relation to homosexual unions and tenancy rights the House of Lords has adopted a liberal stance without resorting to the Strasbourg jurisprudence. Thus in *Fitzpatrick v. Sterling Housing Association Ltd* (1999) 3 W.L.R. 1113 it noted that in conferring rights of succession on persons other than a spouse Parliament had sought to protect from eviction those who had shared their lives with the original tenant in a single family unit. Since the word "family" had been left undefined it fell to the courts to determine which relationships fell within its ambit for that purpose. Having regard to changes in social habits and opinions, associations other

than those based on consanguinity or affinity had come to be recognised as capable of constituting a family, and on an application of the same rationale, a same-sex partner of a tenant was now to be recognised as capable of being a member of a tenant's family for the purposes of the Rent Act 1977.

Surveillance and Data Collection

Key Principle: Secret surveillance by state authorities is tolerable only insofar as it is strictly necessary for safeguarding democratic institutions.

Klass v. Federal Republic of Germany
The applicants claimed violation of Articles 6 and 8 arising from German legislation which permitted the authorities to open their letters and monitor telephone conversations. They had no right to be informed of the surveillance and no recourse to the courts when the surveillance was ended.

Held: (ECtHR) States did not enjoy unlimited power to subject persons to covert surveillance and must provide adequate safeguards against abuse. The surveillance was in accordance with law, was necessary in the interests of national security and contained procedural safeguards. Failure to inform a person that they had been under surveillance was not in principle incompatible with Article 8(2). There was no violation of Article 8 (1979–80) 2 E.H.R.R. 214

Commentary
With reference to Article 8 the court stated that there must be "a balance between the exercise by the individual of the right guaranteed to him under paragraph 1 and the necessity under paragraph 2 to impose secret surveillance for the protection of the democratic society as a whole". It is clear that the main aim of Article 8 is to prevent individuals from being subject to arbitrary interference in their private lives. It is accepted that some interference by the state is necessary. In *MS v. Sweden* (1999) 28 E.H.R.R. 313 the handing over of the applicant's medical confidential records to the Social Insurance Office was an interference

with the right to privacy but it was justified since it was with the legitimate aim of the economic well being of the country in protecting public funds in a claim for compensation.

Malone v. U.K.

The applicant had brought a civil action claiming that interception of his telephone calls during a police investigation was unlawful. The Government denied that his telephone had been tapped but conceded that he did belong to a class of persons liable to telephone interception since he was suspected of dishonestly handling stolen goods. Under existing law the police should have obtained a warrant issued by the Home Secretary before intercepting calls. The applicant claimed a violation of Article 8.

Held: (ECtHR) The law did not make clear sufficiently the scope and manner of exercise of the discretion conferred on police authorities. There was a violation of Article 8 since the interference was not in accordance with law. (1984) 7 E.H.R.R. 14

Commentary

The case led to the passing of legislation which placed such interception on a statutory footing.

Key Principle: **Article 8 may be violated if surveillance by investigatory bodies is not in accordance with law.**

Khan v. U.K.

The applicant had flown to England from Pakistan on the same plane as his cousin who was found on arrival to be carrying prohibited drugs. Later the applicant visited premises which had secretly been bugged by the police drugs squad. In the course of conversation he admitted that he too had brought drugs into the country. The recording of the conversation was the only evidence at the applicant's trial, where he was convicted. He complained that the use made of the recorded conversation breached Articles 6, 8 and 13 of the Convention.

Held: (ECtHR) The bugging could not be considered to be "in accordance with law", since there was no statutory regulation of police surveillance, and Article 8 had been violated. But the use made of the recording had not undermined the fairness of the applicant's trial, since the applicant had been given every opportunity to challenge the admission of the evidence. *The Times*, May 23, 2000

Commentary
The court also considered that there had been a violation of Article 13 of the European Convention on Human Rights since the United Kingdom had not provided any remedy for the breach of Article 8. Thus, irrespective of whether using such evidence makes a trial unfair, it may now be necessary to provide a remedy for breach of Article 8 in such circumstances. Under the Regulation of Investigatory Powers Act 2000 statutory guidelines have been set for state surveillance. Police action in secretly filming defendants in the cell area of a magistrates' court was held to be unlawful and a breach of their right to privacy since it was not in accordance with the law and could not be justified. However a judge had been entitled to admit the film in evidence at the defendants' trial as it had not interfered with the fairness of the trial; see *R. v. Loveridge, The Times*, May 3, 2001. Overall the Strasbourg jurisprudence does not give clear answer on whether video surveillance is a breach of Article 8. In *JS v. U.K.* (1993) the Commission rejected a complaint that covert surveillance by an insurance company was a breach of Article 8. On the grounds that the company's activities did not engage the responsibility of the state.

Immigrants

Key Principle: **Applicants for immigration must demonstrate obstacles to establishing family life in their mother country for refusal of admission by a state to be a violation of Article 8.**

Abdulaziz, Cabales and Balkandali v. U.K.
The applicants were lawfully and permanently settled in the United Kingdom, but under the immigration rules their husbands were refused permission to remain. The applicants claimed violations of Article 8.

Held: (ECtHR) Articles 8 and 14 had been violated on the grounds of sex, since the rules were stricter for husbands who wanted to stay than for wives. Contracting states enjoyed a wide margin of appreciation in determining steps to be taken to comply with the Convention. Although states had a margin of appreciation in determining whether differences in otherwise similar situations required different treatment in law, it was in the last analysis a matter for the court to decide. (1985) 7 E.H.R.R. 471

Commentary
This case illustrates that Article 8 cannot invalidate immigration controls in themselves. The court commented that ". . . the duty imposed by Article 8 cannot be considered as extending to a general obligation on the part of the contracting state to respect the choice by married couples of the country of their matrimonial residence and to accept the non-national spouse for settlement in that country."

Key Principle: **Where a fundamental right, such as family life, was engaged a court would insist that the decision-maker must demonstrate either that his proposed action did not interfere with that right or if it did that considerations existed which might reasonably be accepted as amounting to a substantial objective justification for the interference.**

R. (Mahmood) v. Secretary of State for Home Department
The applicant faced removal as an illegal entrant though by the time the decision was taken to remove him he had married a woman legally settled in Britain and had two children. He claimed that his right to family life had been unlawfully interfered with.

Held: (CA) The decision-maker had to demonstrate either that his proposed action did not in truth interfere with the right, or if it did, that considerations existed which might reasonably be accepted as amounting to a substantial objective justification for the interference. Here there was interference but it was justified in the interests of orderly and fair control of immigration. [2001] 1 W.L.R. 840

Key Principle: **In reviewing executive decisions, including those which concern the effect of Article 8 on a deportation order made against an immigrant with no right to remain in the United Kingdom, the courts will acknowledge the extent of a discretionary area of judgment.**

R. (Isiko) v. Secretary of State for the Home Department

The applicant faced deportation as an illegal immigrant. While under threat of deportation he had married a United Kingdom citizen who had a British child by a previous marriage. Since the child could not lawfully be separated from her father, the effect of the deportation would be to separate the applicant and his wife.

Held: It was lawful under the Convention for a state to have an immigration policy and the mere fact that its implementation could interfere with family life did not render the policy unlawful. The elected government of a country was entitled to lay down and enforce a general policy which did not offend the principle of proportionality. A deportation could be a disproportionate application of the policy, but in the instant case the Home Secretary had been entitled to deport. (2001) 1 F.L.R. 930

Commentary

These two cases raise similar issues of the extent to which the courts would defer to Parliament and executive bodies. In *Mahmood* Laws L.J. stated: "The Human Rights Act does not authorise the judges to stand in the shoes of Parliament's delegates, who are decision-makers given their responsibilities by the democratic arm of the state. . ." In *Isiko* the court recognised that "there will be an area of judgment within which the judiciary will defer, on democratic grounds, to the considered opinion of the elected body or person whose decision is said to be incompatible." This area, however, is an evolving one, see *R. v. Secretary of State for the Home Department, ex parte Daly* [2001] on proportionality as a new ground of review, pp. 28, 135.

Prisoners

Key Principle: **A prisoner's right to uncensored correspondence with a lawyer or judicial body is a fundamental aspect of access to justice.**

Golder v. U.K.

A prisoner in Parkhurst was accused by a prison officer of having taken part in a disturbance. The officer later withdrew the allegation and the prisoner petitioned for the right to consult a solicitor with a view to bringing a libel action against the officer. The Home Secretary refused. The applicant claimed his right of access to justice under Article 6 had been denied.

Held: (ECtHR) The rule of law was scarcely conceivable without the possibility of access to the courts. Though the right was not absolute, the refusal of access to a solicitor had deprived the prisoner of his rights under Article 6 and under Article 8, since it was not necessary in a democratic society that he be prevented from instructing a solicitor. (1979–1980) 1 E.H.R.R. 524

R. (Daly) v. Secretary of State for the Home Department

A prisoner kept in his cell correspondence with his solicitor about his security categorisation reviews and parole. He complained that prison officers following standard procedure had searched his cell in his absence and had examined, though they had not read, the correspondence with the solicitor.

Held: (HL) A prisoner retained, along with the right of access to the courts and to legal advice, the right to communicate confidentially with a legal adviser under the seal of legal professional privilege, that such rights could be curtailed only by express words and then only to the extent reasonably necessary to meet the ends which justified infringement, in this case the need to maintain security, order and discipline and prevent crime. The provision that privileged correspondence should always be examined in the prisoner's absence was void. [2001] 2 W.L.R. 1622

Commentary

The House of Lords here drew the conclusion that proportionality is a matter of law which is a ground of review. The result is likely to be that in cases involving human rights the courts will be more rigorous and robust in reviewing decisions of the executive. (See also p. 28.)

Key Principle: **Any interference with family life had to be justified under Article 8(2) of the Convention.**

R. (P and Q and QB) v. Secretary of State for Home Department
Under a Prison Service Order issued in May 2000, babies with their mothers in prison would be separated from their mothers at the age of 18 months. The applicants appealed against the dismissal of their application for a judicial review of the policy stating that such a policy was a violation of Article 8.

Held: (CA) Article 8 confers not an absolute right to family life but a right to respect for family life. There were necessary limitations on women who were imprisoned. In the great majority of cases mother and child would be separated at 18 months but rare cases would exist where the interests of mother and child outweighed other interests. Appeal for P dismissed and that of Q allowed. [2001] U.K.H.R.R. 1035

Commentary
The case is of interest also because the court stated that it would have reached a different decision had the HRA not been in force. See also *X v. U.K.* (1983) 5 E.H.R.R. 260 and *R. (Lalley) v. Secretary of State for Health* (2001) 1 F.L.R. 406 and *R. (Mellor) v. Secretary of State for Home Department* (p. 142). In the same case, in the Divisional Court, it was considered that the prison service was operating a reasonable balance between the various considerations which was not flawed. It was not for the courts to intervene and run prisons. In this and a number of other cases the courts have adopted a cautious approach to interfering with prison policy.

Key Principle: **In interpreting the Rehabilitation of Offenders Act 1974 the court should uphold its national and international obligations in the field of child protection.**

N v. Governor of Dartmoor prison

The claimant had been convicted of a child sex offence in 1992 and by 1999 this conviction was "spent" pursuant to the Rehabilitation of Offenders Act 1974. In January 2000 he was convicted of drugs offences and sentenced to prison. The governor told the local social services department of the sentence and his release date. He did this following Prison Service instructions which required the governor to minimise the risk that prisoners convicted of sexual offences may present to children under 18 years.

Held: (QBD) On a proper construction of the 1974 Act the governor was committed to disclose the information to social services. It would make it difficult to comply with obligations under the UN Convention on the Rights of the Child 1989 if another interpretation was adopted. Also the impact of Articles 2, 3, 8 compelled the same approach. Owing to their vulnerability children are accorded a special place in terms of international conventions both UN and ECHR. It is their human rights which have a high need of domestic protection. Balancing this with the invasion of the privacy of the applicant the balance was in terms of necessity on the side of the governor's decision. *The Times,* March 20, 2001

Commentary

It is clear that the rights of children and the responsibilities of the authorities to protect them are overwhelming over those of a prisoner who had not offended against children for eight years.

Home and Environment

Key Principle: **Article 8 does not reasonably go so far as to allow individuals' preference as to their place of residence to override the general interest.**

Buckley v. U.K.

A gypsy and her three children lived in caravans parked on land which she owned. The district council refused her retrospective planning permission for the caravans and served a notice requiring their removal from the site.

Held: (ECtHR) The case concerned respect for the applicant's home. There was no doubt that the council's decision was made in pursuit of legitimate aims of public safety and national economic well-being. The means to achieve these aims were not disproportionate and did not exceed the state's margin of appreciation. (1997) 23 E.H.R.R. 101

Key Principle: **Interference with the right to respect for an individual's home must be proportionate.**

Gillow v. U.K.
The applicants had lived for some years in Guernsey and then went to work elsewhere. On their return they were refused permission to occupy the house they owned on the island and prosecuted for unlawful occupation.

Held: (ECtHR) The applicants' right to respect for their home had been interfered with. The housing authority had given insufficient weight to their particular circumstances. The interference was disproportionate to the legitimate aim of keeping the population within acceptable limits and promoting the well-being of the island. (1989) 11 E.H.R.R. 335

Key Principle: **Environmental pollution may constitute an interference with the physical well-being of a person and thus interfere with his private life. It may also deprive a person of the possibility of enjoying the amenities of his home.**

Hatton v. U.K.
The eight applicants all lived in properties near Heathrow Airport. Before 1993 the noise caused by night flying at the airport had been controlled through restrictions on the number of take-offs and landings. But after that date the scheme of control changed, effectively allowing more flights. The applicants claimed violations of Articles 8 and 13 on the ground that judicial review was not an effective remedy.

Held: (ECtHR) In implementing the 1993 scheme the state failed to strike a fair balance between the United Kingdom's economic well-being and the applicants' effective enjoyment of their right to respect for their homes and their private and family lives. There was a violation of Article 8. In the present context the scope of judicial review by the domestic courts was insufficient and there was a violation of Article 13.

Commentary

This case is a considerable victory for those campaigning against noise nuisance and follows in the wake of earlier failed attempts concerning aircraft noise at Heathrow both in the national courts (see *R. v. Secretary of State for Transport, ex parte Richmond* [1996] 1 W.L.R. 1460) and at Strasbourg (see *Powell and Rayner v. U.K.* (1990) 12 E.H.R.R. 355, p. 148). The distinguishing feature in *Hatton*, the court considered, was that the application only concerned night noise in the period subsequent to the earlier unsuccessful applications. It was not therefore a complaint about the operation of the airport in general. The court also found a violation of Article 13. In *Guerra v. Italy* (1998) 26 E.H.R.R. 357 pollution from a chemical factory a mile from the applicant's home provided grounds for a violation of Article 8 since the authorities had not provided relevant information about the risks to health. There is a positive obligation to inform local people about health matters. See also *McGinley and Egan v. U.K.* (1999) 27 E.H.R.R. 1. *Hatton* is being referred to the Grand Chamber of the Court at the time of writing.

Lopez Ostra v. Spain

Villagers living near an industrial plant which treated waste water complained of fumes and smells which made their lives intolerable. They claimed this was a violation of Article 8 as it it damaged their quality of life.

Held: (ECtHR) severe environmental pollution may affect individuals' well-being and prevent them from enjoying their homes in such a way as to affect their private and family life adversely without necessarily seriously damaging their health. (1995) 20 E.H.R.R. 277

Commentary

See also *S v. France* (1990) 65 D.R. 250 where the noise caused by a nuclear power station affected the conditions in a Loire chateau. There was an interference under Article 8 but this was justified as having great benefit to the community.

Victims in Criminal Trials

Key Principle: **Principles of a fair trial may require that on occasions the interests of the defendant are balanced against those of the witnesses or victims under Article 8.**

Doorson v. Netherlands
For facts see p. 84.

Held: (ECtHR) The maintenance of the anonymity of the witnesses limited the ability of the defendant to question them. Although it would have been preferable for the applicant to have attended the questioning of the witnesses it was appropriate to consider that the applicant's interests were outweighed by the need to protect the witnesses. Their life, liberty or security of person may be at stake as may interests coming generally within the ambit of Article 8 of the Convention. There was no breach of Article 6. (1996) 22 E.H.R.R. 330

Commentary
This case, which arose from extreme circumstances, has been cited as illustrating that victims' rights may on occasion be balanced against those of defendants.

7. MARRIAGE AND PROPERTY

Key Principle: **Article 12 of the ECHR: "Men and women of marriageable age have the right to marry and to found a family, according to the national laws governing the exercise of this right."**

Right to Marry

Key Principle: **The chief purpose of Article 12 is to protect marriage as the basis of the family.**

Rees v. U.K.
For facts see p. 127.

Commentary
This case illustrates that the Strasbourg Court has interpreted Article 12 in a somewhat conservative way. The court stated: "The right to marry guaranteed by Article 12 refers to the traditional marriage between persons of opposite biological sex. This appears also from the wording of the Article which makes it clear that Article 12 is mainly concerned to protect marriage as the basis of the family."

Key Principle: **The right to marry does not necessarily include the right to divorce.**

Johnston v. Ireland 1986
For facts and holding see p. 113.

Commentary
This case illustrates the extent of the margin of appreciation afforded to national states in this sensitive area. The approach to divorce illustrated here is tempered by the provision in Protocol 7, Article 5 that spouses within marriage should be treated equally "in the event of a dissolution".

Key Principle: **The ban on homosexual and transsexual marriages is not a violation of Article 12.**

Cossey v. U.K. 1990
The applicant, who is a British citizen, was born in 1954 and registered in the birth register as a male. In her teens the applicant came to realise that she was psychologically female. At 18 she adopted a female name by deed poll and later underwent surgery to have breasts implanted and her genitals altered so that she could have sexual intercourse with a man. She was issued with a United Kingdom passport as a female and became a successful fashion model. But when she sought to marry a man, the Registrar General told her such a marriage would be legally void, since she was classified as a male. The

birth certificate records details as at the birth. She went through a form of marriage in a synagogue but the relationship foundered, and on legal advice she sought divorce on the grounds that the marriage was void as neither party was female. She challenged the refusal of the Registrar to register her as a woman.

Held: Dismissing the application, that though some Member States of the Council of Europe had liberalised their approach to transsexuals, this was by no means universal, and the state had to retain a large margin of appreciation in this field. The prohibition on discrimination in Article 14 did not assist the applicant because she was seeking to use it to introduce into her submissions a concept of proportionality which was already present in the concept of a fair balance between the individual's interests and those of the community at large. However the court was conscious of the seriousness of the problems facing transsexuals and the distress they suffered. Since the Convention always had to be interpreted and applied in the light of current circumstances, it was important to keep under review the need for appropriate legal measures in this area.

Commentary
The court was here following the reasoning also demonstrated in *Rees* (see p. 127). This stand is in accord with English law; the Matrimonial Causes Act 1973 specifies that a marriage is void if the parties are not male and female. The problem for transsexuals is that although they do not have to produce a birth certificate they may be liable for perjury for not declaring impediments to the marriage. In *Cossey* the court acknowledged that it was open to it to take a different approach. Such an approach was recommended in a powerful dissenting judgment. Sweden, Italy and Germany do allow transsexuals under certain conditions to marry a person of their former sex.

———————

Key Principle: **The qualifications on the right to respect for family life recognised by Article 8.2 applied equally to Article 12 rights.**

R. (Mellor) v. Secretary of State for the Home Department
A prisoner serving a life sentence for murder married a member of the prison staff who he had met in prison. When they

married he was 31 years old and given the tariff for his offence expected to spend at least another nine years behind bars. He asked for permission to be allowed to inseminate his wife artificially. The request was refused on the grounds that there was no medical need for artificial insemination and that the marriage had not been tested under normal circumstances and might not last. He was refused leave to seek judicial review and appealed.

Held: (CA) A Prisoner who wished to start a family with his wife had no right to access to facilities for artificial insemination in the absence of exceptional circumstances. Appeal dismissed. [2001] 3 W.L.R. 533

Commentary
The Court of Appeal declared here that imprisonment was incompatible with the exercise of conjugal rights and consequently involved an interference with rights under Article 12 as well as those under Article 8. Leave to appeal to the House of Lords was refused. In exceptional circumstances it could be necessary to relax the imposition of detention in order to avoid a disproportionate interference with a human right but there was no case which indicated that a prisoner was entitled to assert the right to found a family by artificially inseminating his wife. The court referred to *R. v. Secretary of State for the Home Department, ex parte Simms* [2000] 2 A.C. 115 where the House of Lords was expressly interpreting English law in accordance with the Convention on the premise that the relevant principles formed part of the domestic law. It declared that the approach under the Strasbourg jurisprudence and domestic law was the same. The consequences that the punishment of imprisonment had on the exercise of human rights were justifiable providing that they were not disproportionate to the aim of maintaining a penal system designed both to punish and deter. A policy which accorded to prisoners in general the right to beget children by artificial insemination would raise difficult ethical questions and give rise to legitimate public concern.

Peaceful Enjoyment of Possessions

Key Principle: Protocol 1, Article 1—Protection of property: **"Every natural or legal person is entitled to the peaceful enjoyment of his possessions. No one shall be deprived of his** possessions except in the public interest and subject to the conditions provided for by law and by the general principles of international law."

Key Principle: **A balance must be struck between the interests of the community in general and the protection of the individual's right to peaceful enjoyment of his home.**

Sporrong and Lönnroth v. Sweden

In the first case the applicants' property was subject to an expropriation permit which was repeatedly extended until it was finally cancelled since the planned development no longer affected the applicants' building. In the second case an expropriation permit in respect of the applicant's property was set to be valid for 10 years but the project was postponed. The request to have the permit withdrawn was refused and the expropriation permit and a ban on construction ran for eight and 10 years. The applicants claimed a violation of of Protocol 1, Article 1, and Articles 13 and 14.

Held: (ECtHR) There had been an interference with the applicants' properties since they had lost the possibilities of selling them at market prices. There should have been some possibility of review of the permits. The interference was disproportionate and violated Protocol 1, Article 1. (1983) 5 E.H.R.R. 35

Commentary

The court identified three rules in Protocol 1, Article 1. First peaceful enjoyment of property; secondly deprivation of possession only where certain conditions are met; and thirdly state control of use of property by law. Logically the court should establish whether the second and third applied before it could determine if the first was violated. Eight judges issued a dissenting judgment stating there had been no violation of Protocol 1, Article 1 since "the very essence of city planning is to control the use of property including private property in the general interest".

Key Principle: **The right to peaceful enjoyment of possessions may include a right to receive state benefits.**

Cornwell v. U.K.; Leary v. U.K.
Mr Cornwell was a widower with a young son who claimed
that the lack of benefits for his status and the British social
security legislation breached Article 14, Article 8 and Protocol 1
Article 1. Mr Leary was a widower with three young daughters
who was also denied state benefits on these grounds.

Held: (Commission) The cases were admissible on grounds of
violation of Protocol 1, Article 1 and Article 14. *The Times,* May
10, 2000

Commentary
Friendly settlements were reached on the basis that the applicants
should receive benefit as if they were widows until the Welfare
Reform and Pensions Bill was in force. It appears that this
principle applies to compulsory pension schemes (see *Muller v.
Austria* (1975) 3 D.R. 75) as well as those based on employment.
In *Muller,* however, the Commission stressed the differences
between a social security system and the management of a private
pensions system. The operation of the former must include taking
account of political and financial considerations. There have been
a number of challenges to Strasbourg on the basis that some
benefits under United Kingdom law are available to widows but
not widowers.

Key Principle: **The right to enjoyment of possessions may be
infringed in the public interest.**

Mellacher v. Austria
The applicants claimed that legislation reducing the rental
income they could charge on their properties interfered with
freedom of contract and was a breach of Protocol 1, Article 1.

Held: (ECtHR): The rent control legislation pursued legitimate
aims namely reducing disparities between rents for equivalent
flats and controlling property speculation. The legislature was
permitted to interfere with contracts in the public interest. There
was no violation. (1990) 12 E.H.R.R. 391

Commentary
The court followed the case of *James v. U.K.* (1986) 8 E.H.R.R.
123 which held that the leasehold enfranchisement, namely the

right side of a long leaseholders to purchase their landlords' interests was legitimate. The court would not interfere unless the national Parliament was acting without reasonable foundation. Here since Austria's policy of rent control was within its margin of appreciation there was no violation of the right to property. The court has also held that deprivation of a licence is an interference with property rights (*Traktorer Aktiebolag v. Sweden*) as is deprivation of "goodwill" (*Van Marle v. Netherlands* (1986)). The meaning attached to the "public interest" seems to be more generous than that of "necessary in a democratic society". In *James* the court commented:

> "the notion of 'public interest' is necessarily extensive. The court, finding it natural that the margin of appreciation available to the legislature in implementing social and economic policies should be a wide one will respect the legislature's judgment as to what is 'in the public interest' even if the community at large has no direct use or enjoyment of the property."

Key Principle: **The state has a right to enforce such laws as it deems necessary to control the use of property in accordance with the general interest or to secure the payment of taxes or other contributions or penalties.**

Lithgow v. U.K.
The applicants had their assets nationalised and contended that the compensation was inadequate and a violation of Protocol 1, Article 1.

Held: (ECtHR) The standard of compensation for nationalisation was not necessarily to be based on the same criteria as that for compulsory acquisition of land. The Government had acted within its margin of appreciation in setting the compensation rates. (1986) 8 E.H.R.R. 329

Commentary
A number of cases have examined whether the extent of compensation by the state achieves a fair balance between the general interest and that of property owners. See *Holy Monasteries v. Greece* (1995). In *Lithgow*, referring to the level of compensation for the nationalisation of the aircraft and shipbuilding industries, the court declared that it would "respect a national legislature's

judgment in this respect unless manifestly without reasonable foundation".

Key Principle: **Natural or legal persons may only be deprived of property subject to the conditions provided for by law and by the general principles of international law.**

Hentrich v. France

After the applicant had bought some land the Commissioner of Revenue exercised the right of pre-emption because he considered that the sale price was too low and suspected tax evasion. The applicant failed in a challenge to the pre-emption and complained that her right under Protocol 1, Article 1 and Articles 6(1) and (2) of the Convention had been infringed. She also alleged breaches of Articles 13 and 14.

Held: (ECtHR) There had been a breach of Protocol 1, Article 1 and Article 6(1). (1994) 18 E.H.R.R. 440

Commentary

The court recognised that the prevention of tax evasion was a legitimate objective but while the system of the right of pre-emption does not lend itself to criticism as an attribute of the state's sovereignty, the same was not true when its exercise was discretionary and the procedure was unfair. The applicant here bore "an individual and excessive burden" and "the fair balance which should be struck between the protection of the right of property and the requirements of the general interest" was upset. The court has taken quite a passive stance in relation to a state's taxation policy. In *National and Provincial Building Society v. U.K.* (1998) 25 E.H.R.R. 127 it upheld retrospective laws which amended a technical defect whereby applicants were attempting to recover tax they had paid.

Key Principle: **The protection of property is afforded to legal as well as natural persons.**

Wilson v. First County Trust 2001

For facts and holding see p. 19.

Commentary
This case illustrates that businesses have rights as well as individuals. Article 6(1) was engaged as well as Protocol 1, Article 1. This was the first declaration of incompatibility made by the Court of Appeal although others had been made earlier by the Divisional Court.

Environment

Key Principle: **Environmental damage may affect the right to enjoyment of possessions.**

Powell and Rayner v. U.K.
The applicants, who lived near Heathrow airport, complained among other things that noise nuisance had affected their property in violation of Protocol 1, Article 1.

Held: (Commission) This was not an arguable claim since there was no evidence that the value of the applicants' property had been substantially diminished or that aircraft noise had rendered it unsaleable. (1990) 12 E.H.R.R. 355

Commentary
There was a friendly settlement in the case of one applicant whose case was found to be admissible as to violations of Articles 8 and 13 and Protocol 1, Article 1. The Commission forwarded the other two applications to the court with jurisdiction only as to Article 13. It found no violations since there was the possibility of civil action for trespass or nuisance. (For other cases on environmental damage see also pp. 137–139).

8. RELIGIOUS RIGHTS

Key Principle: **Article 9 of the ECHR—Freedom of thought, conscience and religion:**

"1 Everyone has the right to freedom of thought, conscience and religion; this right includes freedom to change his religion or belief and freedom, either alone or in community with others and in public or private, to manifest his religion or belief, in worship, teaching, practice and observance.

2 Freedom to manifest one's religion or beliefs shall be subject only to such limitations as are prescribed by law and are necessary in a democratic society in the interests of public safety, for the protection of public order, health or morals, or for the protection of the rights and freedoms of others."

Range of Beliefs

Key Principle: **Article 9 rights protect a broad range of beliefs and religions.**

Kokkinakis v. Greece 1993
The applicant and his wife were Jehovah's Witnesses sentenced to imprisonment, with a fine in lieu, for proselytising. He complained that this was a breach of his rights under Articles 7, 9 and 10. He argued that no clear dividing-line could be drawn between proselytism and freedom to change one's religion or belief and to manifest it. Religious freedom implied a freedom to bear witness.

Held: The applicant's conviction was not justified by a pressing social need, proportionate to the legitimate aim of maintaining social order or "necessary in a democratic society . . . for the protection of the rights and freedoms of others". (1994) 17 E.H.R.R. 397

Commentary
The court stated in this case that Article 9 ". . . is in its religious dimension one of the most vital elements that go to make up the identity of believers and of their conception of life, but it is also a precious asset for atheists, agnostics, sceptics and the unconcerned." However some political views are not covered by this Article. It does not embrace the concept of a political prisoner. In *McFeeley v. U.K.* it was held that freedom to manifest belief does not include the right of an IRA prisoner to wear his own clothes in prison (see p. 49).

Key Principle: **Organisations as well as individuals may claim the protection of Article 9.**

Chappell v. U.K. 1986
The applicant was a practising druid who complained that the ban on the summer solstice ceremony which had taken place at Stonehenge every year since 1917 was a breach of his right under Article 9 to freedom of religion.

Held: (Commission) The ban was lawful and necessary in a democratic society in the interests of public safety, for the protection of public order or for the protection of the rights and freedoms of others. (1990) 12 E.H.R.R. 1

Commentary
In *Church of X v. U.K.* (1968) 12 Y.B. 306 the Commission indicated that it might be difficult for an organisation to demonstrate a violation of its rights.

Actions

Key Principle: **Actions influenced by a belief are not necessarily manifestations of that belief.**

Arrowsmith v. U.K. 1978
The applicant was imprisoned for incitement to disaffection after distributing pacifist leaflets to soldiers and complained that her right to liberty under Article 5, her right to manifest her pacifist beliefs and her right to freedom of expression had been interfered with.

Held: (Commission) The application was rejected. The applicant's conviction had not violated her Convention rights. (1981) 3 E.H.R.R. 218

Commentary
The court considered that pacifism was a belief and therefore as such entitled to protection under Article 9. Here Article 10 was not violated either, because the state had a legitimate interest in

national security. Again in *Kalac v. Turkey* (1997) App. No. 20704/92 the court found no violation in the removal of a soldier from the military because in fact it was based on his conduct and attitude rather than being a manifestation of his religious belief.

Key Principle: **Conscientious objectors may be afforded protection under Article 9.**

Autio v. Finland

The applicant had done non-combatant national service as a conscientious objector. The law required non-combatant servicemen to spend 240 days more in service than their military counterparts. The applicant complained that requiring him to spend longer in service amounted to discrimination in the enjoyment of his right to freedom of thought, conscience and religion. He further complained that there was no objective or reasonable basis for law, since it was the deliberate intention of the Government to make substitute service more burdensome than military service.

Held: (Commission) The extra length of service was found to be legitimate and proportionate.

Commentary

This issue of conscientious objectors also engages Article 4(3)(6) (see pp. 55–56).

Contractual Status

Key Principle: **An individual in claiming his rights under Article 9 may have to take into account his professional or contractual position.**

Stedman v. U.K. 1997

The applicant, a travel agency worker, was dismissed after 22 months' employment because she refused to accept an amendment to her contract of employment requiring that she work on Sundays. She complained to an industrial tribunal, which declined jurisdiction on the basis that she had been less than two years in the job. The dismissal was upheld by the Court of Appeal. She complained that the exercise of her Christian faith had been interfered with and there were violations of Articles 8, 9, 14 and 6.

Held: (Commission) The requirement that the applicant work a five day week to include Sundays on a rota basis, was not an interference with any of her Convention rights. Her dismissal was not based on her religious convictions. (1997) 23 E.H.R.R. CD 169

Commentary

These two cases illustrate that the European Court of Human Rights is slow to accept the concept of indirect discrimination. It could be argued that insofar as discrimination on religious grounds impacts on a particular racial group it is protected by existing United Kingdom race relations legislation. However some religious groups, such as Rastafarians, are not so protected.

Proportionality

Key Principle: **Any acceptable restrictions on the manifestation of a belief must be in accordance with law, pursuing a legitimate aim as set out in Article 9(2) and be necessary and proportionate.**

R. v. Taylor (Paul Simon)

The appellant was convicted on a guilty plea of possessing cannabis with intent to supply. He was a Rastafarian who claimed he had had the cannabis for distribution and use in a regular act of worship in the temple. Before his guilty plea he had submitted that the prosecution infringed his rights under Articles 8 and 9. In the alternative he argued that the Crown had to prove that the prosecution was a necessary and appropriate response in fulfilment of a legitimate aim. The prosecution accepted that Rastafarianism was a religion. The judge ruled that the drugs had been in use for religious purposes but that although the Convention was engaged, the appellant's rights were qualified by Article 9(2). The appellant appealed against conviction and sentence.

Held: (CA) Convention rights were engaged but the judge's ruling was correct. The jury was not required to examine the issues of proportionality and necessity. The 12 month prison sentence was excessive and was reduced to five months. (2001) *The Times*, November 15

Commentary
Kokkinakis v. Greece (see above) illustrates the importance of the concept of proportionality in the Strasbourg jurisprudence. Its prominence in the Strasbourg cases means proportionality will have increasing importance in English law under the HRA.

Christianity

Key Principle: **By uniquely protecting the Christian religion the English blasphemy laws infringe Article 9.**

Choudhury v. U.K. 1991
The applicant had sought unsuccessfully to prosecute the publisher of Salman Rushdie's Satanic Verses for blasphemy. The English courts ruled that the offence applied only to attacks on Christianity and did not protect Islam. The applicant complained under Article 9 of the Convention that this limited his enjoyment of the right to freedom of religion. He also complained of discrimination under Article 14.

Held: On the Article 9 point, the Commission found no link between freedom from interference with Article 9 rights and the applicant's complaints. Accordingly the discrimination complaint was also rejected.

Commentary
It is arguable that in a pluralist society a criminal law which protects just one religion is not acceptable. An alternative approach is to criminalise attacks on all religions but this could in turn be condemned as an unacceptable infringement of freedom of expression in situations where there was no risk to public order. On the law concerning blasphemy see also *Gay News and Lemon v. U.K.* (1982) 5 E.H.R.R. 123

9. POLITICAL RIGHTS

Freedom of Expression

Key Principle: **Article 10 of the ECHR—Freedom of expression:**

> "1 Everyone has the right to freedom of expression. This right shall include freedom to hold opinions and to receive and impart information and ideas without interference by public authority and regardless of frontiers. This article shall not prevent States from requiring the licensing of broadcasting, television or cinema enterprises.

> 2 The exercise of these freedoms, since it carries with it duties and responsibilities, may be subject to such formalities, conditions, restrictions or penalties as are prescribed by law and are necessary in a democratic society, in the interests of national security, territorial integrity or public safety, for the prevention of disorder or crime, for the protection of health or morals, for the protection of the reputation or rights of others, for preventing the disclosure of information received in confidence, or for maintaining the authority and impartiality of the judiciary."

Key Principle: **Government bodies should be open to uninhibited public criticism.**

Derbyshire County Council v. Times Newspapers
A local authority brought a libel action against a newspaper which had questioned the propriety of its handling of a superannuation fund. On a preliminary point the judge held that the council could sue for libel in respect of its governmental and administrative functions. The decision was reversed in the Court of Appeal and the council appealed.

Held: (HL) Uninhibited public criticism of an elected body was vital in a democracy. The threat of libel actions would inhibit legitimate criticism. It was contrary to the public interest for central or local government institutions to have a common law right to sue for libel. The action would be struck out. [1993] A.C. 534

Commentary
The Court of Appeal applied Article 10 of the ECHR. in finding a local authority cannot sue for libel. The House of Lords held that the common law could determine the issue in favour of protecting free speech.

Key Principle: **Newspapers may have a qualified privilege defence to libel claims where an article, even if it turns out to be untrue, is in the public interest and the product of responsible journalism.**

Reynolds v. Times Newspapers Ltd
The plaintiff, a prominent Irish politician, began proceedings for defamation against the defendants, the publishers of an article about the political crisis in Ireland in 1994. The plaintiff claimed that the article bore the meaning that he had deliberately and dishonestly misled the Dáil. The defendants pleaded qualified privilege. At the trial the jury decided in the plaintiff's favour and he was awarded one penny damages. The Court of Appeal ordered a retrial on the grounds of misdirections to the jury and that the publication was not covered by qualified privilege. The defendants appealed claiming that the law should recognise a generic qualified privilege encompassing the publication by a newspaper of political matters affecting the people of the United Kingdom.

Held: (HL) The common law should not develop a new subject matter category of qualified privilege for all political information. Qualified privilege was available in respect of political information by applying the common law test of whether there had been a duty to publish the material to the recipients and whether they had an interest in receiving it. In the circumstances the publication was not one which should be protected by privilege in the absence of malice. [1999] 3 W.L.R. 1010

Commentary
The paper here failed to benefit from the new defence since the key source had an axe to grant. The case has been hailed as a landmark of press freedom but it has not succeeded often in practice (see *Loutchansky v. Times Newspapers* [2001] 3 W.L.R. 404). Both these cases were decided before the HRA came into effect and show differing approaches to Article 10. In the Court of Appeal judgment in *Derbyshire* Article 10 was involved to resolve uncertainty in the common law but the House of Lords in the same case took the view that the common law rules should reflect the principle that citizens should be exposed to news stories criticising government bodies and politicians. In *Reynolds* the House rejected a defence argument that a new category of qualified privilege "political information" should be created. By contrast, the Strasbourg Court has recognised that the position of a politician is different from that of a private individual (see *Lingens v. Austria* (1986) 8 E.H.R.R. 407). In a case heard after the implementation of the HRA (*Turkington v. Times Newspapers, The Times*, November 3, 2000) the House of Lords held that a press conference was a public meeting and thus protected by qualified privilege under the Defamation Act 1952. The judgment in *Turkington* was not based predominantly on Article 10 or the HRA. Lord Steyn in his judgment invoked the First Amendment to the United States constitution.

Key Principle: **Freedom of expression should be overridden only in extreme circumstances.**

R. v. Secretary of State for the Home Department, ex parte Simms
There was a prohibition on visits to serving prisoners by journalists seeking to investigate whether prisoners had been wrongly convicted save on terms which precluded the journalists from making professional use of the material they collected. The applicant challenged the lawfulness of the ban.

Held: (HL) The more substantial the interference with fundamental rights the more the court would require by way of justification before it could be satisfied that the interference was reasonable in a public law sense. [1999] Q.B. 349

Commentary
The speeches, particularly that of Lord Steyn, assigned great importance to freedom of political speech and drew on American constitutional texts as well as Article 10. Lord Steyn stated:

> "The starting point is freedom of expression. . . Freedom of expression is intrinsically important. It is valued for its own sake. But it is well recognised that it is also instrumentally important. . . It acts as a brake upon the abuse of power by public officials. It facilitates the exposure of errors in the governance and administration of justice of the country."

Key Principle: **Any restrictions on freedom of expression must be prescribed by law and satisfy a pressing social need.**

Sunday Times v. U.K.
The Sunday Times brought the action claiming an injunction upheld by the House of Lords ([1974] A.C. 273) infringed Article 10.

Held: (ECtHR) The interference with the applicants' freedom of expression was not justified under Article 10(2). There was no pressing social need for the injunction. (1979) 2 E.H.R.R. 245

Commentary
This case led to the passing of the Contempt of Court Act 1981.

Key Principle: **Freedom of expression may be restricted if other interests require it and the response is proportionate.**

Arrowsmith v. U.K. 1982
The applicant was a pacifist who distributed a leaflet to soldiers at an army camp urging them to go absent without leave rather than serve in Ireland. She refused to stop after a police warning and was arrested for conduct likely to cause a breach of the peace. She was convicted under the Incitement to Disaffection Act 1934 and sentenced to prison. She alleged breaches of Articles 5, 9, 10(2) and 14.

Held: (Commission) The applicant's pacifism was a belief protected by the Convention but the distribution of leaflets was not a manifestation of belief in the sense of Article 9(1). Her freedom of expression was interfered with but this was justified under Article 10(2). The decision to prosecute her was necessary for the protection of national security and the prevention of disorder in the army. (1978) 3 E.H.R.R. 218

Ahmed v. U.K.
Regulations under the Local Government and Housing Act 1989 restricted the political activities of certain categories of senior local government officers. The applicants were therefore required under the terms of their employment to refrain from engaging in certain political activities. They claimed violations of Articles 10, 11 and Protocol 1, Article 3.

Held: (ECtHR) The regulations pursued the legitimate aim of maintaining the political neutrality of local government officers. There were no violations of the ECHR. (1998) *The Times*, October 2

Commentary
By contrast there was a violation in *Bowman v. U.K.* (1998) 26 E.H.R.R. 1 where the applicant had been prosecuted for distributing views on abortion and embryo experimentation which was in breach of the requirements on election expenses under the Representation of the People Act 1983. The aim of influencing others who are themselves responsible for their actions was an essential and legitimate aspect of the exercise of freedom of expression and opinion, in political and other matters.

National Security

Key Principle: **In cases of national security necessity and public interest disclosure cannot be argued as defences.**

R. v. Shayler
The defendant was charged with offences under section 1(1) of the Official Secrets Act 1989. A preliminary issue was whether there was a defence of disclosure in the public interest or of necessity open to him. He argued that if there were not there would be a breach of Article 10.

Held: (CA) There were no such defences because the fact that the defendant could have disclosed the information to a Crown servant allowed him sufficient freedom. The statutory requirement that damage did not need to be proved when disclosure was by a security service member was justified since, *inter alia*, the lives of operatives were in danger and the United Kingdom might be in breach of its obligations under Articles 2 and 3. [2001] 1 W.L.R. 2206

Commentary

In *R. v. Central Criminal Court, ex parte Bright, Alton and Rusbridger* [2001] 1 W.L.R. 662 the court quashed Special Branch orders made under the PACE to produce material against newspaper editors who had published articles based on revelations by Shayler. It stated that "inconvenient or embarrassing revelations whether for the security services or for public authorities, should not be suppressed".

Protest and Freedom of Expression

Key Principle: **Freedom of expression can encompass actions also.**

Steel v. U.K. 1999

For facts and holding see p. 2.

Hashman and Harrup v. U.K.

For facts and holding see p. 2.

Commentary

In *Steel* the court took the view that the actions of two of the demonstrators constituted "expression" even though they were disrupting the activities of others. In their case the legal action taken against them was a proportionate interference with their freedom of expression. These cases illustrate the close connection between rights under Articles 10 and 11.

Obscenity

Key Principle: **Freedom of expression may include protection of ideas that offend, shock or disturb the state or any sector of the population.**

Handyside v. U.K.
For facts and holding see p. 6.

Commentary
The court maintained that protecting offensive ideas derived from the demands of "that pluralism tolerance and broadmindedness without which there is no democratic society". However how a state operated "the protection of morals" was within its margin of appreciation. In other cases religious sensibilities might be rightfully protected even though this might limit the exercise of artistic freedom (see *Wingrove v. U.K.*).

Libel

Key Principle: **Damages in a libel suit must not be so high as to be a breach of Article 10.**

Tolstoy-Miroslavsky v. U.K.
For facts and holding see p. 107.

Commentary
The court has considered defamation in a number of cases. In *Lingens v. Austria* (1986) the court held that successful private defamation actions brought by prominent politicians were a violation of Article 10. It stated: "Freedom of the press . . . affords the public one of the best means of discovering and forming an opinion of the ideas and attitudes of political leaders. More generally freedom of political debate is at the very core of the concept of a democratic society which prevails throughout the Convention." In this case the court criticised the Austrian defamation law for placing the burden of proof on the defendant to establish the truth of his statement. English law of defamation also places the burden of proof on the defence.

Balancing Rights

Key Principle: **Section 12 of the HRA—Freedom of expression:**

"(1) This section applies if a court is considering whether to grant any relief which, if granted, might affect the exercise of the Convention right to freedom of expression.

(2) If the person against whom the application for relief is made ('the respondent') is neither present nor represented, no such relief is to be granted unless the court is satisfied—

  (a) that the applicant has taken all practicable steps to notify the respondent; or
  (b) that there are compelling reasons why the respondent should not be notified.

(3) No such relief is to be granted so as to restrain publication before trial unless the court is satisfied that the applicant is likely to establish that publication should not be allowed.

(4) The court must have particular regard to the importance of the Convention right to freedom of expression and, where the proceedings relate to material which the respondent claims, or which appears to the courts, to be journalistic, literary or artistic material (or to conduct connected with such material), to—

  (a) the extent to which—

    (i) the material has, or is about to, become available to the public; or
    (ii) it is, or would be, in the public interest for the material to be published;

  (b) any relevant privacy code.

(5) In this section—
    'Court' includes a tribunal; and 'relief' includes any remedy or order (other than in criminal proceedings)."

Key Principle: **Restraints on publication referred in section 12 may be necessary to protect rights under Articles 2 and 3.**

Venables v. News Group Newspapers Ltd
Two boys at the age of 10 had killed the two year old James Bulger. They had been convicted of murder and sentenced to be detained for life. At their original trial the trial judge had made an injunction for an unlimited period forbidding the publication of any information about the two other than their names. In 2001 when they reached 18 years a number of newspapers had applied for clarification. The boys claimed that their rights under Articles 2, 3, and 8 would be at risk if their whereabouts were published.

Held: (Fam. Div.) The protection of confidentiality and the placing of restrictions on the press was correct where not to do so would be likely to lead to serious physical injury or death. [2001] 2 W.L.R. 1038

Commentary
This was an extreme one but it made it clear that the courts can now protect privacy by court order in such cases. Another legitimate basis for press restraint is the protection of national security as the cases arising out of the *Spycatcher* saga showed, see *Observer and The Guardian v. U.K.* (1991) 14 E.H.R.R. 153. The temporary injunctions fell within the state's margin of appreciation in assessing the possible threat to national security. However the confirmation of the injunction after the material was in the public domain because of overseas publication was a violation of Article 10. The specific protection afforded to freedom of expression in section 12 of the HRA will make it more difficult for a pre-trial injunction to be awarded against the press. See also p. 118.

Copyright

Key Principle: **Restriction of the right to freedom of expression in Article 10 could be justified where necessary in a democratic society to protect copyright.**

Ashdown v. Telegraph Group Ltd
The Sunday Telegraph published extracts from Lord Ashdown's *Diaries* including a direct quotation of a minute between Paddy

Ashdown and the Prime Minister. The quoted part was 20 per cent of the whole minute. Ashdown claimed breach of copyright. Summary judgment was granted. *The Sunday Telegraph* appealed.

Held: (CA) Rare circumstances could arise where the right of freedom of expression came into conflict with the protection in the Copyright, Designs and Patents Act 1988 despite that Act's express exceptions. The court was obliged to apply the Act so as to give effect to the right to freedom of expression in Article 10. This required the court to look closely at the facts of individual cases. There was no justification for the extent of the reproduction of Lord Ashdown's own words. Article 10 did not mean that *The Sunday Telegraph* could make money out of this without compensating Lord Ashdown. *The Times*, August 1, 2001

Commentary
The court in this case was concerned with balancing the public interest and the need for commercial confidentiality. It considered it would be rare for the public interest to demand that the form of the work was reproduced.

Protection of Sources

Key Principle: **Freedom of expression may require the protection of journalists' sources of information.**

Goodwin v. U.K.
The applicant, a journalist, had received from a source whose identity he agreed not to disclose, a document about the financial affairs of two private companies. The companies obtained an injunction against publication and an order that the journalist disclose the source. He refused to comply with the order. He also refused to comply when the Court of Appeal varied the order to allow him to place the required information in a sealed envelope lodged with the court. He was found guilty of contempt and was refused a hearing at the Court of Appeal because of his refusal to comply with the order. The publishers and the journalist appealed. The House of Lords held that the Court of Appeal had erred in refusing to hear the journalist since the plaintiff did not oppose his being heard and his appeal

was based on an alleged lack of jurisdiction of the court to make the order. The court had power to order disclosure notwithstanding that the plaintiff's object in seeking it was to identify the source. The potential damage to the complainants' business was great and there was no public interest in publication. The applicant claimed a violation of Article 10.

Held: (ECtHR) The order for discovery was an interference with freedom of expression which was prescribed by law and pursued a legitimate aim. The disclosure order, which merely served to reinforce the injunction, was not supported by sufficient reasons for the purposes of Article 10(2). (1996) 22 E.H.R.R. 123

Commentary
Significantly in *Goodwin* the protection of the commercial interests of the company was a legitimate aim but the measures to achieve them were disproportionate. On protection of commercial interests, see also *Ashdown v. Telegraph Group* (2001) and *Markt Intern GmbH and Klaus Beermann v. Germany* (1990). The growing importance of the protection of "whistleblowers" is now subject to legislation in the Protection of Disclosure Act, and may well raise Article 10 issues.

Extremism

Jersild v. Denmark
The applicant was a television journalist who interviewed some racist youth for a documentary programme. The transmitted programme contained racist and offensive words. The youths were convicted of making racist statements and the applicant was convicted of aiding and abetting their offences. The applicant claimed a violation of Article 10.

Held: (ECtHR) Although the media must not overstep the boundaries which protected others when information and ideas were of public interest the press have a duty to impart them and the public a right to receive them. The documentary had an anti-racist message. Criminal sanctions were not justified and Article 10 was violated. (1995) 19 E.H.R.R. 1

Commentary
Article 10(2) lists the protection of others as a legitimate basis for restricting freedom of expression. This is more specifically cited in

Article 17 which reads: "Nothing in this convention may be interpreted as implying for any State, group or person any right to engage in any activity or perform any act aimed at the destruction of any of the rights and freedoms set forth herein or at their limitation to a greater extent than is provided for in the Convention."

Access to information

Key Principle: **The right to receive information prohibited a government from restricting a person from receiving information that others wished or might be willing to impart to him. It does not give a right of access to secret information.**

Gaskin v. U.K.
The applicant had been placed in the care of the local authority and was boarded with various foster-parents. After he reached the age of 18 the applicant tried to get access to his case records. Some but not all were disclosed. He claimed violations of Articles 8 and 10.

Held: (ECtHR) Persons in the situation of the applicant had an interest in receiving information necessary to know and understand their childhood and an independent authority should finally decide whether access was to be granted where a contributor does not give consent. There was no violation of Article 10 since it does not embody an obligation on the state to impart the information in question. (1990) 12 E.H.R.R. 36

Commentary
United Kingdom governments and authorities wishing to protect information may find support in *Leander v. Sweden* (1987) 9 E.H.R.R. 433. The Swedish Government had refused to give his file to an applicant whom they had turned down for a job on security grounds. It was held that there was no violation since "freedom to receive information contained in article 10 prohibits a government from restricting a person from receiving information that others wish or may be willing to impart to him". It did not confer on an individual right of access to a register containing information on him nor did it embody an obligation on the government to impart such information. See also *Open Door*

Counselling and Dublin Well Women v. Ireland (1992) 15
E.H.R.R. 244. The United Kingdom has now passed a Freedom of
Information Act which does not come into force before 2005.

Freedom of Assembly

Key Principle: **Article 11 of the ECHR—Freedom of assembly
and association:**

   "1 Everyone has the right to freedom of peaceful assembly
      and to freedom of association with others, including the
      right to form and to join trade unions for the protection of
      his interests.

   2 No restrictions shall be placed on the exercise of these
      rights other than such as are prescribed by law and are
      necessary in a democratic society in the interests of national
      security or public safety, for the prevention of disorder or
      crime, for the protection of health or morals or for the
      protection of the rights and freedoms of others. This article
      shall not prevent the imposition of lawful restrictions on
      the exercise of these rights by members of the armed
      forces, of the police or of the administration of the State."

Key Principle: **Prior authorisation or bans for public assemblies is not necessarily a breach of Article 11.**

Platform Artze für das Leben v. Austria 1988
The applicant association comprise the group of doctors who
advocate abortion reform. Cancer demonstrators disrupted their
demonstration. Violations of Articles 9, 10, 11 and 13 were
claimed. The Commission allowed the application on the
grounds of Article 13 only.

Held: (ECtHR) In a democracy the right to counter demonstrate cannot extend to inhibiting the exercise of the right to
demonstrate. The state had a positive duty to ensure that the
right to peaceful demonstration and assembly can be exercised.
The Government had taken positive steps to protect assemblies

and these measures are not in that the quote. There was no violation of Article 11 and therefore no violation of Article 13. (1991) 13 E.H.R.R. 204

Commentary
A broad margin of appreciation is allowed in considering the positive obligations on states but the court was clearly placing the responsibility for any harm that may be provoked on the counter-demonstrators. This case adopts the *Beatty v. Gillbanks* [1882] 9 Q.B.D. 308 robust approach of the common law which was not followed in *Duncan v. Jones* [1936] 1 K.B. 218. However, more recently in *Redmond-Bate v. DPP* [1999] Crim.L.R. 998 a more trenchant rights based approach was adopted. The officer had no right to call upon a citizen to desist from lawful conduct because of a perceived threat from others.

Key Principle: **Prior bans or conditions may be imposed on rallies if they are proportionate to their legitimate aim.**

Rai, Allmond and "Negotiate Now" v. U.K.
The proposed rally was banned by the Department of National Heritage on the advice of the Commissioner of the Metropolitan Police in accordance with government policy that no demonstrations should be allowed in Trafalgar Square if they concerned Northern Ireland. The applicants alleged breaches of Articles 9, 10, and 11.

Held: (Commission) The right to freedom of peaceful assembly is fundamental in any democratic society. There was an interference with rights under Article 11. With regard to the argument that the ban was not based on public order considerations but because it was controversial the Commission considered that there was a legitimate aim involved since the issues were sensitive and complex. The Government had not acted arbitrarily. There were other possible venues. Article 11 was not violated since the restrictions were prescribed by law and necessary in a democratic society. There was no evidence of political discrimination to found the violation on grounds of political opinion. (1995) 19 E.H.R.R. CD 93

Commentary
In finding that the ban was sufficient the prescribed by law the Commission stated: "it is compatible with the requirements of

force the ability that terms which are on their face general and unlimited are explained by executive or administrative statements, since it is the provision of sufficiently precise guidance to individuals . . . rather than the source of that guidance which is of relevance". See also *Steel and others v. U.K.* (p. 2), *Hashman and Harrup v. U.K.* (p. 2) on the varying application of the "prescribed by law" requirement.

Key Principle: **Sanctions against demonstrators must pass the test of proportionality and be necessary in a democratic society.**

Ezelin v. France 1991
The applicant (a lawyer) had been charged with a criminal offence after taking part in a demonstration. The charges were dropped and the Bar Council found no reason to discipline him. However the Court of Appeal imposed a reprimand since he had refused to leave the demonstration or disassociate himself from the offensive and insulting acts which occurred. The applicant alleged breaches of Articles 10 and 11.

Held: (ECtHR) The assembly was lawful; there was an interference with his freedom of assembly which was disproportionate to the legitimate aim of preventing public disorder. (1992) 14 E.H.R.R. 362

Commentary
This is to date the only decision of the court finding a violation of the freedom of assembly guarantee of Article 11. Two judges considered that the interference fell within the state's margin of appreciation. A number of applications have not reached the court since the Commission considered them inadmissible.

Trade Unions

Key Principle: **The right to join a trade union may encompass the right not to join.**

Young, James and Webster v. U.K.
For facts and holding see p. 1.

Held: (ECtHR) The state was responsible under Article 1 for securing Convention rights to its citizens. Article 11 has as one of its purposes the protection of personal opinion and effectively coercing someone to join strikes at its substance. The harm suffered by the applicants was greater than that which was permitted by the aims of closed shop agreements. There was a violation of Article 11; it was not necessary to consider the violations of Articles 9, 10 and 13. (1981) 4 E.H.R.R. 38

Commentary

By contrast in *Sibson v. U.K.* (1994) 17 E.H.R.R. 193 there was no violation of Article 11 after an employer transferred a worker to another place of work because he left one union to join another and other workers would not accept him. There was no risk to his job. In *Young, James and Webster* the court stopped short of completely endorsing the negative right of association which the applicants had advocated but they held that threats of dismissal were a very serious form of compulsion. This judgment has been controversial, trade union protagonists have argued that it shows the preference of the Convention for individualism over collective rights and its lack of regard for the social and economic implications of undermining trade union membership. Such cases illustrate the court's treatment of the complex issue of the closed shop which is no longer protected under English employment law. The difference in the court's decision in the two cases is explained by the fact that in *Young, James and Webster* the workers were threatened with loss of employment because of their refusal to join a union, however in Sibson there was no risk to the applicant's job.

Key Principle: **The right to form and join a union does not include the right to strike.**

Schmidt and Dahlstrom v. Sweden

The applicants were members of trade unions affiliated to one of the main federations representing Swedish state employees. The applicants' unions had called selective strikes not affecting the sectors in which worked the applicants who did not come out on strike. The applicant complained that on the conclusion of new agreements they as members of what were considered "belligerent" unions were denied certain retroactive benefits paid to members of other trade unions and to non-union employees who had not participated in the strike.

Held: (ECtHR) The Convention makes no express distinction between the functions of a contracting state as holder of public power and its responsibilities as employer. Article 11 is binding on the state as employer. Article 11 paragraph 1 presents trade union freedom as one form or special aspect of freedom of association such as the right to retroactivity of benefits. The applicants had retained their personal freedom of association. The Convention safeguards freedom to protect the occupational interests of trade union members by trade union action which must be permitted by Member States. The right to strike is one of the most important of the means available but there are others. Such a right is not expressly enshrined in Article 11 and may be subject under national law to regulation of a kind that limited exercise in certain instances. There was no violation of Article 11 or Article 14. (1976) 1 E.H.R.R. 632

Commentary

The court noted that the 1961 Social Charter only guarantees the right to strike subject to state regulations. In declaring that there was no violation of Article 14 it stated that the principle adopted by the Swedish Government that "a strike destroys retroactivity" was legitimate and it was entitled therefore to pay only those who had not been on strike or supported the strike. In this case the court accepted that the state may regulate the use of industrial action by trade unionists. Thus in *Natfhe v. U.K.* (1998) 25 E.H.R.R. 122 it found no violation of Article 11 in the statutory requirement to give an employer the names of trade union members before strike action was begun.

Key Principle: **Article 11 does not create a right to have a collective agreement concluded.**

Swedish Engine Drivers' Union v. Sweden

The applicant union comprised between 20 per cent to 25 per cent of the eligible railway personnel. The majority of the personnel belonged to the railway men's section of the state employees union (the federations). The applicant complained that the Swedish national collective bargaining office (the Office) concluded it collective agreements only with the federations. The applicant alleged violations of Articles 11, 13 and 14.

Held: (ECtHR) While Article 11 paragraph 1 presents trade union freedoms as one form of a special aspect of freedom of association, the Article does not secure any particular treatment of trade unions or their members by the state such as the right that the state should conclude any given collective agreement with them. The words in the article "for the protection of his interests" showed that the Convention safeguards freedom to protect the occupational interests of trade union members by trade union action the conduct and development of which the contracting states must both permit and make possible. Members of a trade union have a right that the trade union should be heard. The state is free to choose the means which may be by a collective agreement or by other means. There was no infringement of Article 11 paragraph 1. It was not necessary to consider paragraph 2. There was no violation of Article 14 since it was legitimate for the office to want to avoid having an excessive number of negotiating partners. There was no violation of Article 13. (1976) 1 E.H.R.R. 617

Commentary

In other cases the court has ruled that Article 11 does not guarantee any particular union the right to be consulted (*National Union of Belgian Police v. Belgium* (1979-80) 1 E.H.R.R. 578), nor does it create the right to join a particular union in certain circumstances (*Cheall v. U.K.* (1985) 42 D.R. 178). The cases illustrate the limited protection offered to collective as opposed to individual rights in the Convention.

Prisoners

Key Principle: **Solitary confinement is not a violation of the right of association.**

McFeeley v. U.K. 1980
For facts see p. 49.

Held: (Commission) Article 11 does not encompass the right of prisoners to associate with other prisoners in the sense of a right to be in their company.

Commentary

This case involved consideration of a number of Articles, including the nature of a criminal charge under Article 6 in relation to prison disciplinary hearings. The Commission also stated that Article 9 does not guarantee the right to special category status as a political prisoner. Freedom to manifest belief does not include the right of a prisoner to wear his own clothes.

Key Principle: **Convicted prisoners may be disenfranchised.**

R. (Pearson) v. Secretary of State for the Home Department
Several prisoners sought judicial review of the authorities' refusal to register them to vote in parliamentary and local elections. They were disqualified from registering to vote by section 3(1) of the Representation of the People Act 1983. Another prisoner sought a declaration under section 4(2) of the HRA 1998 that section 3(1) of the 1983 Act was incompatible with Protocol 1, Article 3 and Article 14 of the Convention.

Held: (DC) Contracting states had a wide margin of appreciation in imposing conditions on the right to vote. But the conditions should not curtail the rights to such an extent as to impair their essence or remove their effectiveness, should be imposed in pursuit of a legitimate aim and the means employed should not be disproportionate or thwart the free expression of the opinion of the people in the choice of the legislative. Parliament had taken the view that convicted prisoners in custody had forfeited their right to have a say in the way the country was governed. (2001) *The Times*, April 17

Commentary
The Representation of the People Act 2000 gives remand prisoners and mentally ill patients, other than those convicted and in custody, the right to vote.

Limitations

Key Principle: **Article 11 rights may be restricted in their application to the armed forces, the police, and civil servants.**

CCSU v. U.K.
Mrs Thatcher as Minister for the Civil Service issued an order in Council withdrawing from employees at the Government Com-

munications Headquarters (GCHQ) the right to belong to a trade union. There had been no prior consultation with the unions or the employees. The Civil Service unions and six employees sought judicial review on the ground that the minister was under a duty to act fairly by consulting those affected. The single judge granted a declaration that the order was invalid, the Court of Appeal found for the minister and the applicants appealed. The House of Lords held that merely because the minister was exercising a prerogative power she was not immune from judicial review or freed from the duty to act fairly. However the Government had shown that the decision was based on considerations of national security which outweighed fairness. The unions complained to the Commission.

Held: (Commission) The complaint was manifestly ill-founded. There had been an interference with the applicants rights under Article 11 paragraph 1 but this was justified by the exceptions provided for under paragraph 2. The employees at GCHQ were "members of . . . the administration of the state". The measures taken were in accordance with national law and the restriction could be interpreted as covering a complete prohibition of the right under Article 11. It was not clear whether the restriction in this area had to be proportional but even if this were so in cases of national security a wide margin of appreciation was allowed to contracting states. GCHQ was vulnerable to industrial action and given its vital functions the drastic measures taken were not arbitrary. (1987) 50 D.R. 228

Commentary

The Commission considered that it could get no guidance on this issue from the international instruments. The International Covenant on Civil and Political Rights 1966 did not restrict the rights of employees in state administration whilst the International Covenant on Economic Social and Cultural Rights 1966 did do so. The International Labour Organisation (ILO) however did find the United Kingdom to be in breach of the relevant Article of the ILO treaty on freedom of association. The judgment was controversial since it approved outlawing membership of a union, not just the right to take industrial action. The Blair Government has restored the right to join a union to the GCHQ employees.

Key Principle: **Discrimination against public sector employees on political grounds may be a violation of Articles 10 and 1.**

Vogt v. Germany

A teacher had been sacked from her post because her active membership of the Communist Party was considered incompatible with her duties. She claimed violations of Articles 10 and 11.

Held: (ECtHR) Articles 10 and 11 were violated. (1995) 21 E.H.R.R. 205

Commentary

This was a landmark decision. In the earlier cases of *Glasenapp v. Germany* (1987) 9 E.H.R.R. 25 and *Kosiek v. Germany* (1987) 9 E.H.R.R. 328 the court had held that a condition that applicants for civil service jobs uphold the constitution was not a violation of the Convention. They were distinguished because the court considered there that the applicants had not been qualified whereas here the applicant had been a teacher for seven years before the dismissal. There were no security considerations and the ban was disproportionate. The ban made no distinction according to rank. There was no right of recruitment to the civil service in the Convention but "this does not mean . . . that a person who has been appointed as a civil servant cannot complain on being dismissed if that dismissal violates one of his or her rights under the Convention". The court also considered that German schoolteachers were "not members of the administration of the State", see also *Devlin v. U.K.* p. 111.

Professional Bodies

Key Principle: **Professional bodies do not necessarily fulfil the "common goal" requirements of voluntary association.**

Le Compte, Van Leuvan and de Meyere v. Belgium

The first applicant, a doctor, was struck off the medical register; he did not comply with the order and was sentenced in a criminal court to imprisonment and a fine. The second and third applicants were also doctors who were suspended from practice by the relevant professional body. All three applicants alleged violations of Article 6(1) in that the hearings were not public, and Article 11.

Held: (ECtHR) The word "association" presupposes a voluntary grouping with a common goal. The non-voluntary and public nature of most professional regulatory bodies excludes them from Article 11. There were violations of Article 6(1) in that the cases were not heard publicly by a tribunal competent to determine all aspects of the matter. (1982) 4 E.H.R.R. 1

Commentary
The court noted that totalitarian regimes have resorted to the compulsory regimentation of the professions by means of closed and exclusive organisations taking the place of the professional associations and the traditional trade unions. The authors of the Convention intended to prevent such abuses. There were in Belgium several associations formed to to protect the interests of medical practitioners and which they were completely free to join or not. This safeguards rights under Article 11.

Free Elections

Key Principle: **Protocol 1, Article 3—Right to free elections: "The High Contracting Parties undertake to hold free elections at reasonable intervals by secret ballot, under conditions which will ensure the free expression of the opinion of the people in the choice of the legislature."**

Mattieu-Mohin and Clerfayt v. Belgium
The French-speaking applicants complained that as voters living in Flemish administrative districts they could not elect French-speaking representatives to the regional assembly and that as elected representatives they could not sit in that assembly whereas Dutch-speaking voters and elected representatives in the same municipalities could. They alleged violations of Protocol 1, Article 3 and Article 14.

Held: (ECtHR) There were no violations of either article. The state had a positive obligation to ensure free elections. Protocol 1, Article 3 protected the right to vote and the right to stand for election but these rights were not absolute and could be subject to implied limitations. Such limitations must not impair the very essence of the right. (1988) 10 E.H.R.R. 1

Commentary
This is to date the only case considered under Protocol 1, Article 3. Referring to the rights to vote and to stand for election the court stated that "since article 3 recognises them without setting forth in express terms, let alone defining them, there is room for implied limitations". See also *Ahmed v. U.K.* (p. 158). The court made it clear in *Mathieu-Mohin and Clerfayt v. Belgium* (1987) that states enjoy a considerable margin of appreciation in this area and the courts will only interfere if the essence of the protected rights is interfered with. In *R (Robertson) v. Wakefield Metropolitan Council, The Times,* November 27, 2001, the applicant complained that the electoral registration officer had failed to respect his wish that his name and address should not be sold on to commercial organisations. The Administrative Court held that the officer had acted contrary to the Data Protection Directive and to Article 8 and to Protocol 1 Article 3 of the European Convention on Human Rights. The claimant had established an unjustified, disproportionate restriction on his right to vote.

10. SOCIAL RIGHTS— DISCRIMINATION

Education

Key Principle: **Protocol 1 Article 2—Right to Education: "No person shall be denied the right to education. In the exercise of any functions which it assumes in relation to education and to teaching, the State shall respect the right of parents to ensure such education and teaching in conformity with their own religious and philosophical convictions."**

Key Principle: The state's respect for the right of parents to ensure education and teaching in conformity with their own religious and philosophical convictions should be accepted in so far as it is compatible with the provision of efficient instruction and the avoidance of unreasonable public expenditure.

Campbell and Cosans v. U.K.
The applicants had no realistic alternative but to send their children to Roman Catholic Schools where children were beaten. Following a minor disciplinary infraction the son of one of the applicants refused with his parents' support to accept a beating and was suspended. The school refused to readmit him until the parents accepted that in future he could be beaten . Both parents claimed breaches of Article 3 and Protocol 1, Article 2.

Held: The duty to respect parental convictions cannot be overrriden by the alleged necessity of striking a balance between differing viewpoints. The state's policy to move gradually towards abolition of corporal punishment was not in itself sufficient to comply with its duty. There were violations of both sentences of Protocol 1, Article 2. (1982) 4 E.H.R.R. 293

Commentary
The case illustrates that state must respect the religious and philosophical convictions of parents although there are limits to this respect. The state may satisfy the Article by a pluralist approach to education and it may claim financial restraint. The parents had to demonstrate that there was a demonstrable causal connection between their belief and the reason they object to what the state is doing. Opposing corporal punishment did amount to philosophical convictions. (See also p. 53).

Key Principle: The right to education encompasses the development and moulding of the character and mental powers of pupils.

Campbell and Cosans v. U.K.
For facts see above.

Commentary

Here the court also acknowledged the importance of taking a broad view of the meaning of education in a pluralist society. It referred to ". . . a weighty and substantial aspect of human life and behaviour, namely the integrity of the person, the propriety or otherwise of the infliction of corporal punishment and the exclusion of the distress which the risk of such punishment entails."

Key Principle: **There is no positive obligation on a state to provide education in a minority language.**

Belgian linguistic case (No. 2)

French speaking parents living in Flemish speaking regions of Belgium wanted their children educated in French. However no state schools in the area taught in French. The parents alleged that their rights under Articles 8, 9, 10 and 14 of the Convention and under Protocol 1, Article 2 had been violated.

Held: (ECtHR) In principle a law which appears to comply with a Convention Article might in fact constitute a breach when that Article is read together with Article 14, if the law is discriminatory. Article 14 is an integral part of every other Article. It does not prohibit all differential treatment, only that differential treatment which is not objectively and reasonably justified. Protocol 1, Article 2 and Article 14 did not require the state to deliver education in the language of the parents' choice. (1979–80) 1 E.H.R.R. 252

Commentary

It is significant that the wording of the Articles is restrictive. It requires that the state shall not deny rather than that it should positively guarantee or respect the right to education. The burden is on the individual to prove interference not the state to defend non-provision. The Article gives the state discretion on the scope of its provision since it refers to "the exercise of any function which it assumed in relation to education and to teaching". Similarly the Article is primarily concerned with elementary education. There is no obligation to ensure that certain groups such as prisoners or foreigners are given access to more specialist education such as university education. Nor is the state required to fund home or private education, though it may regulate them. *Family H v. U.K.* (1984)

Key Principle: **Although the state must not pursue an aim of indoctrination that does not respect parents' religious and philosophical convictions it may impart knowledge of an indirectly or directly religious or philosophical kind .**

Kjeldsen, Busk Madsen and Pedersen v. Denmark

The applicants alleged violations of Protocol 1, Article 2 and Articles 8, 9 and 14 on the grounds that the compulsory sex education introduced by statute in Danish state schools was contrary to their beliefs as Christian parents.

Held: (ECtHR) Parents are not permitted to object to the imparting of information of a religious or philosophical kind because otherwise all institutionalised teaching could be impracticable. Information must be conveyed in an objective, critical and pluralist manner and must not amount to indoctrination which did not respect parents' religious and philosophical convictions. The legislation did not affect the right of parents to enlighten and advise their children. There were no violations of the Convention. (1979–80) 1 E.H.R.R. 711

Commentary

A key feature of this case was that the state could not avoid its responsibilities by referring to the legality of private schools. If it did so this would lead to the position that only the rights of wealthy parents were "respected".

Discrimination

Key Principle: **Article 14 of the ECHR—Prohibition of discrimination: "The enjoyment of the rights and freedoms set forth in this Convention shall be secured without discrimination on any ground such as sex, race, colour, language, religion, political or other opinion, national or social origin, association with a national minority, property, birth or other status."**

Sex Discrimination

Key Principle: **The margin of appreciation accorded to states in relation to sex discrimination is very narrow.**

Schmidt v. Germany

There was a requirement in the region where the applicant lived for all male but not female adults to perform local fire brigade duties or to pay a financial levy. The constitutional court held that there was an objective justification for the difference. In fact women did serve in local fire brigade so it was the levy which constituted the difference of treatment on grounds of sex. The applicant alleged breaches of Articles 4 and 14 in relation to forced labour and with Protocol 1, Article 1 in relation to taxation.

Held: (ECtHR) There were violations of Article 14 in conjunction with the other two Convention rights. Reasons behind difference of treatment on grounds of sex must be very strong. As equality advances so the roles of the sexes must be re-addressed. (1994) 18 E.H.R.R. 513

Commentary

In this case the difference of treatment concerned a financial levy not physical activity so the court did not pronounce on whether there were intrinsic differences which made women less suited to certain kinds of work.

State benefits and discrimination

Key Principle: **Traditional practices and roles of men and women may not necessarily justify difference in treatment in relation to state benefits.**

Van Raalte v. Netherlands

Unmarried childless women but not men over the age of 45 were exempted from having to pay contributions towards child benefit. The applicant, an unmarried childless man over the age of 45, claimed the exemption breached Protocol 1, Article 1 in conjunction with Article 14. The state claimed that the difference was because women over 45 rarely procreate but men do.

Held: (ECtHR) There was no objective reasonable justification for the different treatment. Women could claim child benefit by reason of adopting, fostering or becoming step mothers. There was a violation of Article 14 in conjunction with Protocol 1, Article 1. (1997) 24 E.H.R.R. 503

Commentary
By contrast, in *Petrovic v. Austria* (1999) 4 B.H.R.C. 232 the court found no violation when a father was denied parental leave for a month. The court observed that such benefits originally applied only to mothers and have gradually been extended to fathers as society's view changed. Here the difference (which had subsequently been removed by legislation) was within the state's margin of appreciation.

Homosexuals

Key Principle: **Discrimination cannot be justified by a fear that some members of society might draw misguided conclusions from its removal.**

Sutherland v. U.K.
For facts see p. 125.

Held: (Commission) There was a violation of Articles 8 and 14.

Commentary
See also pp. 124–126 for the protection afforded to homosexuals under ECHR.

Racial Discrimination

Key Principle: **Racial discrimination may amount to a type of degrading treatment under Article 3.**

East African Asians v. U.K.
For facts see p. 51.

Held: (Commission) The legislation which imposed immigration controls on most East African Asian citizens was racially motivated and amounted to degrading treatment under Article 3 in relation to the British subjects. In relation to the six applications by "protected persons" the legislation did not distinguish between categories of British protected persons on any racial basis and there was no violation. The refusal to grant residence to the applicants whose wives had already been granted permanent residence was a violation of Articles 8 and 14 since the applicants had been subjected to discrimination on the ground of sex in relation to their family lives. (1973) 3 E.H.R.R. 76

Commentary
By contrast in *Abdulaziz, Cabales and Balkandali v. U.K.* (1985) 7 E.H.R.R. 471 the court disagreed with the Commission's finding that there had been a violation of Article 3 when the husbands of three women immigrants who were lawfully and permanently settled in the United Kingdom were not allowed to join them. The rules then in place applied more strictly to men wishing to join their partners than to women or nationals of the EU Member States. It held that the difference of treatment complained of did not denote any contempt or lack of respect for the personality of the applicants and was not designed to, and did not humiliate or debase but was intended solely to achieve the aims of the policy. It could not therefore be regarded as "degrading" .There was accordingly no violation of Article 3. There had been a violation of Articles 8 and 14, along with Article 13, on the ground of sexual discrimination. However the rule was not racially discriminatory.

Under Article 14 there is a guarantee of freedom from "degrading treatment" which could apply to racial discrimination but in this case the Commission considered racial discrimination under Article 3. In 2000 the 12th Protocol was adopted providing a freestanding "equal treatment guarantee" under which discrimination by the state in any rule of conduct is prohibited. It will come into force when ratified by 10 states; the United Kingdom has not signed it. Article 13 of the treaty of Rome empowers the council, after consultation with the Parliament, to combat discrimination based on sex, racial or ethnic origin, religion or belief, disability, age or sexual orientation.

Disability Discrimination

Key Principle: **Article 14 has no independent existence if the facts of a case do not fall within another Convention right.**

Botta v. Italy
The physically disabled applicant found there were no adequate facilities at his seaside holiday resort. Under Italian law private beaches are required to facilitate the access of disabled people. There were no proceedings against the local authorities for failing to enforce the relevant law. The applicant alleged violations of Articles 3, 5, 6(1), 13 and 14. The Commission declared admissible the applications in relation to Articles 3, 5, 8 and 14.

Held: (ECtHR) On the facts the case did not fall under any Convention right. Article 14 could not apply. (1998) 26 E.H.R.R. 241

Smith v. U.K.
The applicant was a gypsy who argued that United Kingdom law criminalised her way of life such as her rejection of permanent accommodation. The offence of parking a caravan outside a designated area was discriminatory since it applied only to gypsies. She alleged breaches of Articles 8, 11 and 14.

Held: (Commission) The applicant had not proved that the law had a real and direct effect on her way of life so as to breach Articles 8 or 11. There was no violation therefore under Article 14. (1993) 18 E.H.R.R. CD 65

Commentary
In relation to some groups, such as the disabled and gypsies, the rights under the ECHR. are less comprehensive than those under national legislation, see for example the Disability Rights Commission Act 1999 and the Race Relations Act 1976 under which gypsies are protected as a minority group.

Political Opinions

Key Principle: **A difference of treatment in relation to political opinion may be justified if it pursues a legitimate aim.**

184 Nutcases—Human Rights

McLaughlin v. U.K.

The applicant was a member of Sinn Fein. He complained that the directive issued by the Home Secretary in 1988 prohibiting the BBC and ITV to broadcast spoken words of any person who represented or appeared to support a proscribed organisation was a breach of Articles 10, 13 and 14. He was the victim of political discrimination since the ban did not apply to supporters of certain other political parties.

Held: (Commission) The interference with freedom of expression was prescribed by law and had a legitimate aim of combating terrorism. It was not disproportionate and although it would have little direct effect upon the amount of terrorism, it was legitimate to deny publicity to certain causes. There was no breach of Articles 10 or 14. The differential treatment was justified. (1994) 18 E.H.R.R. CD 84

Commentary

In *Arrowsmith v. U.K.* (1978) 3 E.H.R.R. 218 the Commission found no violation of article 14 since the difference of treatment with other protesters was justified. They had heeded police warnings to cease distribution of leaflets (see also p. 150).

Jury Bias

Key Principle: **Racial discrimination by juries violates the ECHR.**

Sander v. U.K.

For facts see p. 73.

Held: (ECtHR) A tribunal must be impartial from a subjective as well as an objective point of view. Racial comments by jurors was a very serious matter in today's multi-cultural European societies. This was not redressed by the judge's redirection to the jury. The judge should have reacted in a more robust manner. There was a violation of Article 6(1). (2000) 8 B.H.R.C. 2791

Commentary

The case was distinguished from the earlier case concerning jury discrimination, *Gregory v. U.K.* (1998) 25 E.H.R.R. 577. In the latter there had been no breach of the "impartial tribunal" guarantee in a trial of a black defendant when a jury member had passed a note to the trial judge that read "jury showing racial overtones. One member to be excused". It was considered in *Sander* that there were two grounds of distinction from *Gregory*. First in *Gregory* the complaint of bias was more vague and imprecise, and secondly in *Sander*, but not in *Gregory*, the applicant's counsel had insisted throughout the proceedings that the discharge of the jury was the only proper course.

11. REMEDIES

An Effective Remedy

Key Principle: **Article 13 of the ECHR—Right to an effective remedy: "Everyone whose rights and freedoms as set forth in this Convention are violated shall have an effective remedy before a national authority notwithstanding that the violation has been committed by persons acting in an official capacity."**

[N.B. This Article is not incorporated into English law by the HRA 1998.]

Key Principle: **In assessing whether to award damages and if so how much the court will take into account the seriousness of the violation of the victim's human rights.**

Aksoy v. Turkey
The applicant was arrested as a suspected member of the Kurdish revolutionary movement, PKK. He was stripped naked, his hands were tied behind his back and he was strung up by his arms, a so-called "Palestinian hanging", while electrodes were applied to his genitals and water was thrown over him. He was severely beaten and tortured for four days. He made an application to the Commission but before it could be heard he

was shot dead, allegedly by a government agent. His application was continued by his father, the prosecuting authority
having failed to investigate the torture and murder of his son.

Held: (ECtHR) States were under a particular obligation to
investigate incidence of torture. The prosecutor's decision to
ignore the applicant's complaint was tantamount to undermining the effectiveness of any remedy available to the applicant.
Since Turkish law did not provide proper compensation, the
applicant would be awarded compensation consisting of medical expenses and loss of earnings, together with non-pecuniary
damages, including an element to reflect the aggravated nature
of the Convention breach. (1997) 23 E.H.R.R. 553

Commentary
This was an extreme case. Claims for punitive damages do not
usually succeed apparently because they are not compatible with
the aim of full restitution (see below).

Key Principle: **Article 41—Just satisfaction: "If the Court
finds that there has been a violation of the Convention or the
Protocols thereto, and if the internal law of the High Contracting Party concerned allows only partial reparation to be made,
the Court shall, if necessary, afford just satisfaction to the
injured party."**

Key Principle: **There must be a causal link between the
violation and the loss.**

H v. U.K.
The applicant had successfully claimed a violation of Article 6(1)
over proceedings to obtain access to her child who was in local
authority care lasting two and a half years. She now claimed
damages for *inter alia* loss of the relationship with her daughter
and loss of the opportunity to have children.

Held: (ECtHR) There was no identifiable causal connection
between some aspects of the claim and the violation since it
could not be said that a speedier conclusion would have led to a

different relationship with her daughter. However it was not possible to exclude the possibility that speedier proceedings might have had a different outcome. There was therefore a loss of real opportunities and the court was prepared to award damages for this. (1988) App. No. 9580/81

Commentary
The United Kingdom Government had reached a settlement with the applicant over costs.

Damages and the Human Rights Act

Key Principle: **Limitation periods in civil claims must be interpreted in the light of Article 6.**

Cachia v. Faluyi
A wife and mother had been killed in a road traffic accident in 1988 while the children were minors. At the time of the accident the husband sought damages and issued a writ both under the Fatal Accidents Act 1976 and on behalf of the estate under the Law Reform Miscellaneous Provisions Act 1934. The writ was never served. When the children were 21 in 1997 they commenced proceedings. The limitation period did not run till they reached majority but under section 2(3) of the Fatal Accidents Act 1976 not more than one action shall lie for and in respect of the same subject matter of complaint. It was submitted that Article 6 gave the children right of access to the court to claim compensation for their loss of dependency.

Held: (CA) It was necessary to construe the term "action" as meaning "served process". In this way the legislation was given effect in a way which was compatible with Convention rights. [2001] 1 W.L.R. 1966

Commentary
This case demonstrates the effect of the HRA in personal injury cases. To date there have been no awards of damages in an English court specifically under the Act. The Government had resisted including Article 13 in the HRA arguing that section 8 of the Act provides for effective remedies. During the passage of the Bill-through Parliament it was conceded that the courts may have

regard to Article 13 when applying Section 8(4) of the HRA 1998 which reads: "In determining (a) whether to award damages, or (b) the amount of an award, the court must take into account the principles applied by the European Court of Human Rights in relation to the award of compensation under Article 41 of the Convention." Section 8(4) refers only to the principles applied by the Strasbourg Court rather than their application to individual assessment of damages. In the Court of Appeal decision in *Heil v. Rankin* [2001] Q.B. 272, a personal injury case, Lord Woolf viewed the court's task as "limited to providing fresh guidelines so as to give effect to well established principles as to the objective which should be achieved by an award of damages. Full compensation was the main objective, applying to non-pecuniary as well as to pecuniary loss. The use to which the claimant would put the money was irrelevant." The English law on this is undergoing development. The Law Commission has considered the application of the principle of full restitution under the HRA and concluded that the English courts were not bound in every case to follow Strasbourg precedents and would determine the majority of cases according to the normal common law rules for determining damages. Lord Woolf has commented that the absence of Strasbourg principles as to damages would allow the English courts to develop their own principles within the statutory framework.

Judicial Review

Key Principle: **Judicial Review may be an adequate remedy for the purposes of Article 13.**

Soering v. U.K.
For facts see p. 45.

Held: (ECtHR) The "death row phenomenon" constituted torture or inhuman or degrading treatment but the fact that a United Kingdom court would have jurisdiction to set aside a decision on these grounds was an effective remedy. (1989) 14 E.H.R.R. 248

Commentary
The Strasbourg Court has addressed this question in a number of cases and has come to differing decisions. For example in *Smith*

and Grady v. U.K. (2000) 29 E.H.R.R. 548 (p. 7) it stated that in those circumstances judicial review was not an effective remedy and in fact the domestic courts had taken a similar position. See also *Chahal v. U.K.* (1997) 23 E.H.R.R. 413 (p. 45) where the court held there had been a violation of Article 13 and there were no effective remedies available since neither the advisory panel nor the courts had the power to review the Home Secretary's deportation decision. This was a case where national security was involved. There is a particular problem where private bodies are involved because they are not generally subject to judicial review.

Inadequate Redress

Key Principle: **The Police Complaints Procedure is not an adequate remedy for the purposes of Article 13.**

Khan v. U.K.
For facts see p. 88.

Held: There had been a violation of the applicant's rights under Article 8 and since the Police Complaints Authority was not a sufficiently independent body to protect individuals from abuse by the authorities there was a breach of Article 13. (2000) 8 B.H.R.C. 310

Commentary
The case illustrates that even though there may be procedures for redress under national law they may not be acceptable under Article 13. In *Silver v. U.K.* (1983) 5 E.H.R.R. 347 there was a violation of Article 8 in relation to a prisoner's correspondence. The court stated that neither the prison board of visitors, nor the Parliamentary Commissioner for Administration, nor judicial review nor the Home Secretary were able to supply effective remedies to comply with Article 13.

Key Principle: **Article 13 can be satisfied even where the domestic remedy is limited by statute.**

Powell and Rayner v. U.K.
For facts see p. 148.

Held: (ECtHR) Although liability for nuisance and trespass resulting from aircraft noise had been excluded by statute, the exclusion was not absolute and it was for a court to decide whether it applied. Unreasonable aircraft use and noise could still form the basis of a domestic action for trespass or nuisance so there was no violation of Article 13. (1990) 12 E.H.R.R. 355

Commentary
For treatment of exclusion of liability under the HRA where Convention rights are involved, see *Marcic*, p. 32.

Responsibilities of Contracting States

Loizidou v. Turkey
The European Court of Human Rights had awarded damages to the applicant, a Greek Cypriot, against the Turkish Government in respect of her claims relating to property in Kyrenia which had been seized by the Turkish administration in North Cyprus. The court found that the Turkish action had violated her Convention rights. The Turkish Government refused to pay the award, stating that it could be paid to the applicant in the context of a global settlement of all property cases in Cyprus. The committee of ministers in 1999 strongly urged Turkey to comply, but Turkey did not.

Resolution (Committee of Ministers): Turkey's obligation to abide by judgments of the court is unconditional . . . Turkey has had ample time to fulfil in good faith in the present case its obligations. Failure on the part of a High Contracting Party to comply with a judgment of the Court is unprecedented. The refusal of Turkey to execute the judgment of the Court demonstrates a manifest disregard for its international obligations, both as a High Contracting Party to the Convention and as a member State of the Council of Europe. In view of the gravity of the matter, strongly insists that Turkey comply fully and without any further delay. Resolution DH (2000) 105, 24 July 2000.

Commentary
This case indicates the limitations of the enforcement procedures where a state is recalcitrant. Under Article 46 responsibility for supervising the execution of the ECtHR's judgments rests with the Committee of Ministers. Decisions of the Committee of Ministers are published as resolutions. Defendant states can issue measures

which include payment to the applicant, reopening of proceedings, reversing the verdict, discontinuing the expulsion proceedings and implementing changes to legislation. In a resolution issued in June 2001 the Committee noted that in order to give effect to the decision in *Jordan, Stephen v. U.K.* (App. No. 30280/96) the Government had introduced amending legislation and made a payment to the applicant in respect of costs and expenses. It had thus addressed the violation that the Strasbourg Court identified when it had found faults in the courts-martial system.

Key Principle: **An application can be struck out of the list if the court is satisfied that the parties have reached a satisfactory agreement.**

Duyonov v. U.K.
The applicants were Georgian refugees who had intended to seek asylum in Canada. Instead they were put ashore in Gibraltar, where they surrendered to the immigration authorities. The governor authorised their removal under a local immigration control ordinance. They brought habeas corpus proceedings on the basis that the section of the ordinance used against them applied only to people had been fined or imprisoned in the courts. The case was on its way to the Privy Council. There was no provision for legal aid before the Privy Council. The applicants claimed that was a breach of their rights under Article 6. Before the case reached Strasbourg the Government and the applicants reached a friendly settlement and legislation was introduced to allow legal aid in Privy Council proceedings. The Government applied for their action to be struck out.

Held: (ECtHR) The court was satisfied that the settlement was based on respect for human rights as defined in the Convention and the case should accordingly be struck out of the list. App. No. 36670/97

Commentary
The United Kingdom Government agreed to pay the applicants £5,000 to cover pecuniary and non-pecuniary damages and costs. Account should be taken of the fact that damages would be paid out of public funds not out of a bottomless purse. Section 8(3) of

the HRA makes it clear that damages should not be nominal since the purpose is to achieve "just satisfaction", nor for the same reason should they be exemplary or punitive. In a recent controversial decision, *Akman v. Turkey* 2001 (App. No. 37453/97) the court struck out an application from a father who alleged his son had been unlawfully killed by the Turkish security services. He claimed violations of Articles 2 and 13. It was not in dispute the son had been killed by the security services but the authorities claimed he had opened fire. No investigation took place into the death. The Turkish Government had issued a declaration of regret at the death and an *ex gratia* payment of £85,000 was paid.

Key Principle: **Neither Article 13 nor the Convention in general requires that contracting states implement the provisions of the Convention in any particular manner.**

Swedish Engine Drivers' Union v. Sweden
For facts see p. 170.

Held: (ECtHR) The Swedish Labour Court examined the union's complaints and took into account Sweden's international obligations. Neither Article 13 nor the Convention lays down for contracting states any given manner for ensuring within their internal law the effective implementation of any of the provisions of the Convention. There was no violation of Article 13. (1976) 1 E.H.R.R. 617

Commentary
The court stated that in these circumstances it was not called upon to rule whether, as the Swedish Government had contended and the Commission affirmed, Article 13 is applicable only when a right guaranteed by another Article of the Convention has been violated. However in a later case, *Silver v. U.K.* (1983) 5 E.H.R.R. 347 the court made it clear that it was not a precondition of Article 13 that there was an actual breach of another Convention right. It was necessary for the applicants to have "an arguable claim" to be entitled to seek an effective remedy. The court referred to the 1961 Social Charter of the Council of Europe. Article 6 paragraph 2 of that document affirmed in the court's view the voluntary nature of collective bargaining.

Key Principle: Article 5(5): "Everyone who has been the victim of arrest or detention in contravention of the provisions of this Article shall have an enforceable right to compensation."

Benham v. U.K.
The applicant, who was unemployed and not drawing benefit, failed to pay community charge. He was denied legal aid before the magistrates, who decided that his failure to pay was wilful and committed him to prison. The Queen's Bench Divisional Court later held that the magistrates were wrong to have done so because prison should only be used for non-payers who had the means to pay. The applicant complained that the denial of legal aid was a violation of Article 6.

Held: (ECtHR) In view of the severity of the penalty risked by the applicant and the complexity of the applicable law, the interests of justice demanded that, in order to receive a fair hearing, Mr Benham ought to have benefited from free legal representation during the proceedings before the magistrates. There was no breach of Article 5(1) and thus no right to compensation. (1996) 22 E.H.R.R. 293

Commentary
Article 5 is the only Article which gives a right to compensation where there is a breach. The key question here was whether the decisions of the magistates' court were within its jurisdiction or in excess of jurisdiction. The former were effective unless or until they were overturned by a superior court whereas the latter would be null and void from the outset. The court here felt able to distinguish *R. v. Manchester City Magistrates' Court, ex parte Davies* (1989) on the basis that there the magistrates had failed altogether to carry out the inquiry required by law whereas in the present case the magistrates had addressed the question but had reached a finding which could not be sustained on the evidence. It should be noted that Article 13 has no application where Article 5(4) or Article 6(1) are in issue. These have specific requirements.

Exclusion of Evidence in Criminal Trials

Key Principle: **Police and Criminal Evidence Act, s. 78:**

"(1) In any proceedings the court may refuse to allow evidence on which the prosecution proposes to rely to be given if it appears to the court that, having regard to all the circumstances, including the circumstances in which the evidence was obtained, the admission of the evidence would have such an adverse effect on the fairness of the proceedings that the court ought not to admit it.

(2) Nothing in this section shall prejudice any rule of law requiring a court to exclude evidence."

Key Principle: **Exclusion of evidence may result from breach of a Convention right.**

R. v. Looseley
For facts see p. 91.

Held: (HL) The court had to balance the need to uphold the rule of law by convicting and punishing criminals with the need to prevent the police from acting in a manner which constituted an affront to the public conscience or offended ordinary notions of fairness. It would be unfair and an abuse of process if a person had been lured, incited or pressurised into committing a crime which he would not otherwise have committed. [2001] 1 W.L.R. 2060

Commentary
In this case the House of Lords articulated the approach of the courts to the application of section 78 of the PACE. It made it clear the possible remedies for breach of the Convention in criminal proceedings, namely a stay of prosecution or exclusion of evidence. Human rights points should be raised in the criminal proceedings themselves not in parallel judicial review proceedings. Only the higher courts can issue a declaration of incompatibility as a species of remedy (see Chapter 2).

12. THE EUROPEAN UNION AND HUMAN RIGHTS

General Principles

Key Principle: **The general principles of European Union law enshrine fundamental human rights.**

Matthews v. U.K.

A Gibraltar resident did not have the opportunity of voting in the elections for the European Parliament because of the limited scope of Annex 2 of the European Community Act on Direct Elections 1976. She claimed that the right to free election under Protocol 1, Article 3 of the ECHR had been infringed.

Held: (ECtHR) There was a breach of the Protocol. [1999] 28 E.H.R.R. 361

Commentary

Prior to this decision the Court of Human Rights had considered all cases concerning European Community law to be inadmissible. This decision paves the way for the intervention of the Court of Human Rights into areas previously thought to be within the jurisdiction of the European Court of Justice (ECJ). The Court of Human Rights accepted that the European Community could not be challenged because it was not one of the high contracting parties to the ECHR. (see *Re Accession of the Community to the European Human Rights Convention*, Opinion 2/94, below). However, the United Kingdom, since it had participated in making the Council Decision, had violated the ECHR. If the court had not acted the applicant would have lacked a remedy for a serious violation of the fundamental human right.

Key Principle: **The European Community could not accede directly to the ECHR.**

Re Accession of the Community to the European Human Rights Convention Opinion 2/94

The ECJ was asked to give its opinion of whether the Community could accede directly to the Convention.

Held: (ECJ) There was no legal basis in the Treaty of Rome to permit accession. [1996] 2 C.M.L.R. 265

Commentary

The European Community would have to amend the treaty of Rome in order to accede. Article 6 of the Treaty on European Union 1997 (The Treaty of Amsterdam) states that "the Union shall respect fundamental rights for the protection of Human Rights and Fundamental Freedoms signed in Rome on November 4th, 1950 and that they result from the constitutional traditions, common to the Member States, as general principles of Community law". However this is a non-justiciable Article. In the face of pressure for a more coherent human rights approach the heads of state and government decided at the Cologne summit in July 1999 that an E.U. charter of fundamental rights would be drawn up, including general rights of liberty and equality as well as economic and social rights. The Charter was proclaimed at the Nice conference in December 2000 but was not made part of the subsequent treaty.

Key Principle: **The Convention is a source of Community law.**

Firma J Nold v. Commission

The applicant's argued a violation of his property rights after a Commission decision, revising the terms of trading for coal wholesalers, meant that he could not meet the requirements.

Held: (ECJ) Property rights were protected by German constitutional provisions and the Convention. Such rights could be limited in the public interest and the applicant could not be protected in the absence of fundamental errors or flaws in procedure. [1974] 2 C.M.L.R. 338

Commentary

All Member States of the European Community had signed the Convention by 1974.

INDEX